ISLAMIC JIHAD,
CULTURAL MARXISM AND THE TRANSFORMATION OF THE WEST

W. AUGUST MAYER

To my mother Madeline, who gave me life and to my wife Patricia who gave me hope.

CONTENTS

ISLAMIC JIHAD, CULTURAL MARXISM AND THE TRANSFORMATION OF THE WEST

W. AUGUST MAYER

SAN FRANCISCO, CA - PIPELINEMEDIA

CHAPTER ONE - PROLOGUE

"...I hate ingratitude more in a man than lying, vainness, babbling, drunkenness, or any taint of vice whose strong corruption inhabits our frail blood..." [William Shakespeare: Twelfth Night, Act III. Scene IV]

Some nights, the ghost of Caesar Rodney haunts me, his pitiable grief a soft wailing beast deprived of blessed death. Vanity, drunkenness...the taint of strong corruption; ingratitude exceeds them all. His gift we cavalierly ignore.

Rodney, pale and weak from facial cancer and emphysema dragged himself from bed and upon the hard leather saddle. Giving his mount its head...it well knew the trail to Philadelphia, where his delegation stood deadlocked and waiting.

A chilling thunderstorm was his only companion. Resolute not to see the promise of a unanimous Congressional declaration of liberty die by his hand, he would not allow it to tumble back into the void of divisiveness, not now, not ever...

The rider's vote broke the Delaware delegation's impasse on the question of independence, as through his considerable effort the state cast its vote for liberty. That it was the 12th to do so made his action even more remarkable because it wasn't essential to the ratification process; the Continental Congress had already dealt with that possibility, ruling that that passage would require but nine votes.

Though poignantly heroic, he wasn't alone in his bravery and willingness to "bear any price."

George Washington, James Madison, Benjamin Franklin, Thomas Jefferson, John Adams, Alexander Hamilton; all involved in the deliberations which led to independence pledged their lives, their fortunes, their sacred honor and so attested as they signed the document - an act of high treason and one not lightly undertaken.

Many did indeed pay dearly:

William Ellery, a member of the Rhode Island delegation, saw his ancestral home set ablaze by the British. Nearly a dozen of the other signatories to the Declaration suffered similar fates, family estates ransacked, then put to the torch or otherwise wrecked.

New Jersey's Richard Stockton - a philanthropist, who donated part of his family's land holdings as the site for what would later become Princeton University - was imprisoned, brutally mistreated and nearly starved to death. He lost everything, dying an invalid from cancer at the age of 51. Four of his associates were similarly apprehended as prisoners of war; the Brits weren't noted for treating the American rebels kindly.

Nine died during the conflict.

Typical of the self-sacrificing ethos surrounding the revolution, Thomas Nelson, Jr., a member of the Virginia delegation, knowing that his home was being occupied and used as a British command center, ordered it burned to the ground.

His too was a pauper's death.

Over 10,000 Colonists died while held in British captivity, most of them on the infamous prison ships such as the HMS New Jersey, where the treatment was brutal. Many more died in this manner than as a result of the actual fighting. The total number of Americans killed during the war, of all causes - disease being primary among them - is impossible to determine with any degree of certainty; estimates range from a low of 40,000 to as many as 60,000, with about 25,000 Redcoats also falling.

In the colonies, life was always hard. It became even more so during the upheaval; suffering was a given, General Washington's tattered army was woefully underfunded given its mission of liberating a nation which itself was divided in its loyalties.

Money was tight, but the Colonists were every bit as ingenious as they were impetuous.

Much of the war was financed by a few wealthy Americans. Especially noteworthy was Robert Morris who gave selflessly from his personal fortune, especially early in the war when the need to field an army was most acute. In this regard Morris had but one peer - Chaim Solomon whose provision of financial aid at the end of the war was especially pivotal. Between Morris and Solomon, the two established a covert funding stream [as well as a sort of a lend-lease arrangement for military hardware] with France. Acting much like our own Federal Reserve, the Continental Congress ran the printing presses with abandon. The resulting flood of Continental fiat money caused widespread inflation, a tradeoff which had to be made.

Despite these efforts, so little in the way of "specie" was available that Washington constantly worried that his troops might starve to death.

In 1780 he drafted one of a succession of dispatches to Congress:

> "It is with infinite pain that I inform Congress that we are reduced again to a situation of extremity for want of meat. On several days of late, the troops have been entirely destitute of any, and for a considerable time past they have at best, at half, a quarter, an eighth allowance of this essential article of provision." [source, The life of General Washington: first president of the United States, Volume 1 p. 370]

Petitioning Congress to provide a sustainable method of paying for the necessities of war ran headlong into reality; taxation under the Articles of Confederation was the province of the states alone.

The buckskin clad rebels weren't at first blush nearly the equal of Britain's skilled professional warriors, at the time the best, most battle-hardened soldiers in the world. Actually, the men Washington led weren't really an army at all; though many were highly accomplished hunters and marksmen, they initially lacked the discipline and tactical understanding needed to bind them into an effective fighting force. Cohesion was instilled through constant drilling tempered with a bit of coercion - when required - including instances when units were posted at the ready to maintain battle lines and prevent desertions in the face of fire.

Though the recruits were generally young they were transformed by the nature of their mission. Those who perished along with those who survived to witness the final victory endured a level of hardship and privation which is hard to imagine - their yearning for liberty outweighed the terrible price it demanded; war is an ugly thing.

As the truism goes, history is written by the victors, but for every story recorded about these remarkable men, there are countless others which will never be told - their sacrifice rewarded with anonymity.

What manner of principle could instill this level of devotion in a movement, the outcome of which was problematic at best? Within that question lies the unique premise upon which America is based, the individual right to manage his affairs free from the meddling of a despotic ruler.

In the space of a few words, the Declaration's author Thomas Jefferson justified the pursuit of liberty and freedom as a sacred duty, "to assume among the powers of the earth, the separate and equal station to which the Laws of Nature and of Nature's God entitle them."

To the Founders, the laws of "nature's God" could be rationally discerned through reason, so much so that they were "self-evident." The rights which were endowed by the Creator and thus beyond the province of man to remove, were enumerated as "life, liberty and the pursuit of happiness."

It is only because men are fallible creatures, easily given to poor judgment, vice or other misdeeds, that it becomes necessary for them to enter into social agreements or compacts in order, "to secure these rights," and thus, in liberal democracies, governance flows upwards from the people.

> "Governments are instituted among Men, deriving their just powers from the consent of the governed."

Self-rule was and remains an ambitious undertaking; it had never before been tried on a national scale. Its strengths were also the source of potential weakness, requiring citizens to be informed, ethical, vigilant and involved in the process of managing their own affairs. Quite literally they held dual responsibilities - governors as well as the governed.

> "Only a virtuous people are capable of freedom. As nations become corrupt and vicious, they have more need of masters." - Benjamin Franklin

> "Neither the wisest constitution nor the wisest laws will secure the liberty and happiness of a people whose manners are universally corrupt. He therefore is the truest friend to the liberty of his country who tries most to promote its virtue, and who...will not suffer a man to be chosen into any office of power and trust who is not a wise and virtuous man." - Samuel Adams

The need to remain morally righteous was reinforced by a powerful devotion to a living Christian faith so palpable it would be alien to most contemporary Westerners. Contrary to claims by revisionist historians, the Founders were not deists.

To the people of that time religion was a deadly serious matter.

> "Of all the dispositions and habits which lead to political prosperity, religion and morality are indispensable supports.... And let us with caution indulge the supposition that morality can be maintained without religion." - George Washington

Within the relatively short span of our history, a million and a half members of America's Armed Forces have given their lives: many more have been maimed and countless millions of families and their communities have had to bear the pain of irreparable loss in pursuit of a singular goal, that of preserving these liberties. Three-quarters of a million - all of whom deserve equal honor - perished in the nation's most costly and bitter contest, which finally resolved the question of slavery.

Though slavery inextricably became interwoven into the Civil War, do not be mistaken, preserving the Union was Lincoln's only non-negotiable demand; he would have sacrificed nearly anything else in order to prevent the nation from being torn asunder.

> "My paramount object in this struggle is to save the Union, and is not either to save or destroy Slavery. If I could save the Union without freeing any slave, I would do it, and if I could save it by freeing all the slaves, I would do it, and if I could save it by freeing some and leaving others alone, I would also do that. What I do about Slavery and the colored race, I do because I believe it helps to save this Union, and what I forbear, I forbear because I do not believe it would help to save the Union." [Abraham Lincoln, A Letter to Horace Greely, the New York Times, August 22, 1862]

Lincoln knew what hung in the balance, aware of the unique nature of the American experiment - the Revolutionary war had been fought only 80 years previous, those wounds still bled as was reflected in his plurality victory in the 1860 election where he was unable to garner even 40% of the popular vote.

The President's library and personal reading list contained many volumes dealing with U.S. history, including George Bancroft's, History of the United States an unapologetically patriotic retelling of the country's founding as well as Jonathan Elliott's Journal and Debates, a History of the Federal Constitution [source, Robert Bray, What Abraham Lincoln Read].

So trusted was Bancroft that he served in the Lincoln cabinet as Secretary of the Navy, overseeing the great transition which was brought about when almost overnight, iron clad vessels dramatically rendered wooden navies obsolete. It was Bancroft who was chosen to eulogize the late president before congress.

The 16th President knew that a nation such as ours might only come along once. With that promise removed he saw only darkness, "We shall nobly save, or meanly lose, the last best hope of earth." [source, Abraham Lincoln, Second Annual Message to Congress, Dec. 1, 1862, the New York Times]

The fleeting and cyclical nature of freedom and liberty has long been recognized. But it has been seldom expressed with more insight and grace than by Alexander Fraser Tytler, Lord Woodhouselee, a Scottish nobleman, professor of history and general man of letters.

Serendipitously, it was written in 1787, the year in which the Constitution became the supreme law of the land, evidence perhaps of some small measure of celestial guidance:

"From bondage to spiritual faith
From spiritual faith to great courage
From courage to liberty
"From liberty to abundance
From abundance to complacency
From complacency to apathy
From apathy to dependence
From dependence back into bondage"

This is the treasure of our American legacy, unique in the history of the world. Would it not be the ultimate act of hubris for this generation to casually throw away such a singularly fragile bequest?

We appear to be well on our way.

Paraphrasing Churchill, an iron curtain has descended across the West which is merrily engaged in transitioning from dependence "back into bondage." Today, nearly 230 years after this passage was written, the republic is staring down an existential threat, the nature of which might not have come as a surprise to Dr. Tytler.

Legacy, tradition, an endless manifest of debts unpaid; America is as much an idea as it is an expanse of territory, its coasts bound by the two largest oceans on the planet. Being the only true flower of Continental Europe, but one free of the physical and psychological traumas a thousand years of habitation inevitably produces, perhaps America is more idea than substance - in one sense a wispy, thin-spun vase fragile enough for the reliquary, in another, a battering ram that brought tyrants to their knees.

Now gloved, that hard fist no longer even commands respect, let alone fear.

Bound in a web of our own design, the West has been delivered captive into a strange, alien land where the basest, most misguided conception of freedom has been turned against it in unimaginable ways, victimized by its very spirit of tolerance.

Long gone are the days when our foe quartered troops in the homes of citizens, levied outrageous taxes and imposed its will from afar. It's been a quarter of a millennium since a foreign potentate sat astride our liberty and freedom.

But we have constructed a far more cunning and malevolent enemy with our very hands. This one walks our streets undetected, delivers our newspaper, teaches our children, represents us in Congress, leads us in hollow prayer…

"Stand your ground. Don't fire unless fired upon, but if they mean to have a war let it begin here." - Captain John Parker, Lexington Green, April 19, 1775

CHAPTER TWO - STARRY NIGHT

"...they will always judge me or talk about me from different points of view, and you will always hear the most divergent opinions about me. And I blame no one for it, because relatively few people know why an artist acts as he does. But in general, he who searches all kinds of places to find picturesque spots or figures - holes and corners which another passes by - is accused of many bad intentions and villainies which have never entered his head." - Vincent van Gogh, Brussels, 2 April 1881

November 2, 2004

To his neighbors it was a familiar but still mildly comedic sight, the fleshy 47 year-old Theo van Gogh, cigarette jutting petulantly from his lips, leaving his home in Watergraafesmeer and peddling off on an "old man's bicycle" - straw basket attached - towards his office at Column Productions, his film company.

Van Gogh was the great grandnephew of Dutch painter Vincent van Gogh. In appearance though, he differed physically in many ways from his ancestor. Especially absent was Vincent's hawk-like haunted visage and gaunt profile. In its place, Theo loomed a compelling and at times imposing figure. He had the look of a patrician, ruddily complected and raw-boned with tousled blond ringlets of hair scattered across his head in no particular pattern.

While one could hardly escape the gaze of those piercing grey green, deeply set eyes which shone with a combined fury and child-like passion, as his opponents inevitably discovered, above all there was van Gogh's acid tongue.

Along with inheriting more than a bit of Vincent's artistic sensibility and inspiration perhaps he as well bore the mark of his ancestor's demons. Judging from outward appearances van Gogh's life was chaotic, he pitched and swayed, swirling from project to project - actor, director, polemicist, bon-vivant…at all times the libertine whose calculatingly offensive personality ably served a finely-crafted sense of outrage that both aided and encumbered him.

Van Gogh's caustic jibes and printed tirades were legendary, but mostly reserved for public figures, especially those whom he considered pompous and overly proud. He particularly detested the studied correctness of the political class, whom he called "salon socialists" and others whom he felt to be phonies or moral cowards, of which there are many in Holland.

Organized religion did not escape his invective. Christians were at times blistered with scorn. He derided them as simple minded, "followers of that rotten fish from Nazareth." He served up the same to Dutch Jews, even going so far as having once described the imagined "wet dream" of a Jewish adversary, in which he claimed she wanted to be "fucked by Joseph Mengele."

Vicious stuff, sometimes of such mean intent as to be irredeemably vile. Nonetheless, he delighted in pushing the limits of tolerance in a country known for its extreme open-mindedness and questioning attitude. In van Gogh's world, there were more than enough objects deserving of excoriation, to be incised with language so over the top as to be comedic and brutal simultaneously.

What was language to him but another tool, a bare canvas upon which to splash, gouge and model toward one end - communication, to be able to break through the clatter of life?

If this latter day van Gogh's renderings contained over-saturated, garish colors, so much the better to make a point. In his mind subtlety made little headway in a universe distinguished by its unsubtle nature and a country which was changing before his eyes, unshockable as if by edict, yet shocking in its constitution, sublime acquiescence and passivity.

His most incendiary language however was reserved for members of Holland's large Muslim immigrant population, many of whom had come from Northern Africa, especially Morocco. For the fundamentalists among them, those who had tended towards fanaticism and especially the bellicose imams, he used the term "geitenneukers" - goat fuckers - a coinage that had been in limited slang usage but which he gleefully popularized.

However, as was usually the case, van Gogh's blunt criticism contained a more reasoned core, though couched in his usual combativeness:

> "It's not my fault that some fellow-citizens hang to the fundamentally uncivilized faith of a little-girl-fucker who roamed the desert in 666. We may thank Allah that there are hundreds of thousands of reasonable Muslims in this country who don't blemish His name. But they too are intimidated by the apparently pittoresque village officers of Mecca's thought police, who try to sell the imagined blood that steams from their sewers by whining about 'respect.'"

Van Gogh's life was a celluloid crucible of his own forging; a documentary - starring himself - constantly running inside his head. Even now, preoccupied as he was in early November with the air turning cold, as early fall mornings in Holland often are, the scenes flowed in a way no hard-copy edit could even approach - the proud van Gogh, no the imperial van Gogh, Agamemnon's champion, a later-day Achilles, borne on an armored chariot, spiked projections jutting from its axles, poised to harvest the rotten fish's disciples and lay low all that deserved it.

This dawn saw Theo rushing off to the studio to work on what would be his twenty-fifth film, "6/5" which chronicled the assassination of Dutch MP Pym Fortuyn - another iconoclast, proudly gay and a van Gogh idol, whom he inelegantly referred to as that "divine bald head," in his rough but in this case, loving parlance - murdered two years earlier, on May 6, 2002 by a vegan, animal rights extremist and Muslim apologist, Volkert van der Graaf.

Fortuyn was as critical of the modern Dutch experience with Muslim immigrants as was van Gogh, but his criticism was more cerebral than that of the film maker's, more studied. This was understandable given that Fortuyn was a PhD whose zest for inquiry caused him to stray from his Marxist roots to an eventual embrace of capitalism.

About Fortuyn's assassination, a political act that stopped a movement, van Gogh penned:

> "...The rage of Van Dam, Kok, Van Kemenade, Melkert and all those other salon socialists was probably also related to the notion that Left seemed to lose its natural dominance in the public debate in the weeks before the sixth of May. It was as if Fortuyn would break the power of the paralyzing Sixties in one blow. The gentlemen panicked, as for the first time in Dutch history the outcasts of the nation threatened to actually come into power. That wasn't part of the plan. Fortuyn was the hated face of this impending revolt. Left was flooded away and had only its worn jargon left. A lot of babbling about 'extreme right', 'racism', 'reliving fascism' and silently creating the climate in which murder becomes an act of heroism. There is something perverse about the fervor with which Volkert van der G. [Fortuyn's murderer] was denounced a 'madman'. A madman excuses our guilty conscience from the thought that we might have overreacted a little bit..."

Though Holland considers itself a freethinking country, like most left-wing institutions and societies, it is supremely intolerant of alternative viewpoints.

Call it situational tolerance.

One aspect of this intellectual flatulence is seen in Europe's anti-hate speech laws which have given governments that supreme prosecutorial tool, criminalization of thought. Though this legislation ostensibly grew out of the Nazi experience and the desire to prevent its recurrence, the blindness of dealing with such a complex phenomenon with reflexive legislation can't be underestimated.

It is particularly ironic that a draconian, near Nazi level of control has been brought forth as a method of preventing the resurrection of the twisted iron cross.

The Universal Declaration of Human Rights [adopted post-Nuremberg in 1948] was the precedent upon which all of the anti-hate laws draw their sustenance. As legal scholar Jieskje Hollander observed [when commenting on the specifics of article 10(2) of this legislation] though the UDHR generally recognized free speech, it was qualified. Unrestrained free speech - the genuine article - wasn't similarly protected.

> "This paragraph gives us a range of reasons for which the right to freedom of speech can and should be restrained. The right to express oneself freely comes with certain special duties and responsibilities...If speech is used recklessly or with malicious intent it will threaten the security of society in various ways, it will threaten the constitutional state and it will harm the individual." [see, Hate Speech, a Historical Inquiry into its Legal Status, Jieskje Hollander, p. 31]

We are left with the irreducible absurdity of defining free speech in such a manner as to suppress it.

In effect therefore, Holland's vaunted laissez faire exterior houses a totalitarian heart - free-thinking reduced to thinking in a state or societally approved manner.

It was around this rotting core that both Fortuyn and van Gogh railed, seeing their countrymen silenced - many voluntarily wearing a ball-gag - into inaction against what they saw as an invasion by a hostile horde.

Two years after the murder of Fortuyn, van Gogh assembled a 10 minute film that proved to be so controversial that it seemed he was intentionally courting disaster.

That work titled *Submission,* [a literal translation of the Arabic word Islam] featured a heavily veiled Muslim woman, with only her eyes showing, suffering in a stylized manner the Shari'a approved sentence for fornication, 100 lashes. Van Gogh used semi-nudity to enhance the obscenity of the punishment as did the covering of her body with Quranic verses, elaborately stylized as inky black tattoos. Throughout the work, other women are similarly treated for various infractions of Islamic religious law.

This juxtaposing of what to many if not most traditional Muslims is the sacred alongside the profane, generated the outrage that van Gogh sought. That the script was co-written by a fallen Muslima, Ayan Hirsi Ali, made the degree of societal discomfort all the more delectable one might surmise.

Was that short film, publicly broadcast only months before, on van Gogh's mind as he rolled along the street in front of Amsterdam's East Borough office? Though, unfortunately that query can never be answered, we surmise that it couldn't have been far from his consciousness.

What is known however was that as he traversed the space in front of the political office complex, the stadsdeelkantoor, on his creaky bicycle he wasn't alone. He was being stalked, hunted by a determined young Muslim, Mohammed Bouyeri, outraged beyond all measure by the very existence of works like *Submission.*

Bouyeri, then a 26 year old native-born citizen and the son of Moroccan immigrants had earlier joined a cell of the Dutch terrorist Hofstadgroep [aka Hofstadnetwerk].

It modeled itself along the ideological lines of the Takfir-wal-Hijra, drawing inspiration from Egypt's Muslim Brotherhood

16

[though technically, the noun takfir is applied to one who has been expelled from Islam as an apostate or guilty of gross heresy/blasphemy. Historically this has been used as a juridical method to provide scriptural grounding to allow warfare between nominally Muslim nations or peoples]. Bouyeri had served time in Dutch prisons where it's believed that he adopted the Takfir ideology, which is to lay low, blend in and assume an unremarkable lifestyle, then at the critical point, when the kufr guard is down, to leap, slash and annihilate.

Bouyeri charged on foot towards the startled van Gogh, firing a 9mm HS 2000 semi-auto pistol as he closed the distance between himself and his victim, rapidly directing nine rounds towards the stunned bicyclist, seven of which found their way home.

Van Gogh struck, crashed to the ground as if thrown. Though seriously wounded and bleeding profusely, he remained conscious and lucid, pleading with Bouyeri while on his knees, "please don't do it, don't do it, we can still talk about it."

Imagine the shock, the clever van Gogh…words, his beautifully sinister tool, utterly failing him.

Remorselessly, Bouyeri advanced, deed not yet completed, a long kitchen type knife now in hand. He then administered the brutal coup de grace, butchering van Gogh on the sidewalk like an animal, slicing through his throat all the way to the spinal column, nearly severing the film maker's head.

An onlooker called out saying, "You can't do that," but Bouyeri replied in chilling calmness, uttering a political warning, "Yes, I can. Now you know what's coming to you."

Calmly and methodically, the killer then pinned a rambling, five-page manifesto - a declaration of war against the governments of the West and Dutch politicians - on the now lifeless body, contemptuously plunging the murder weapon and another knife for good measure, through the note and deep into the right side of van Gogh's barrel-like chest.

Translated, the note is a chilling manifesto of exultation, a calling to arms of Bouyeri's comrades.

"I surely know that you, O America, will be destroyed - I surely know that you O Europe, will be destroyed - I surely know that you O Holland will be destroyed - Drenched in blood these are my final words - Pierced by bullets - As I had hoped - I am leaving a message behind - For you...the fighter - The tree of Tawheed is waiting - And longing for your blood - Take up the challenge - And Allah will help you overcome - He gives you the garden - In place of this earthly rubble - To the enemy I also have something to say - You will certainly try to resist - But even if you go on a Tour of the world - Death is Lurking right behind you - The Horsemen of DEATH are at your heels - And the streets will be covered red with Blood - To the hypocrites I say will end with this - Wish for DEATH or else keep quiet ...and sit..."

At trial Bouyeri confessed to the ritual murder, adding that he wanted to become a martyr for his religion. Unrepentant, he promised similar mayhem if released. Furthermore he testified that he felt commanded by the Qur'an to "chop off the head" of anyone who insulted Islam or its prophet.

The assassination was declared to be an act of terrorism, making his eventual release unlikely. Reflecting the surreal, clipped-tone nature of the ultra-high security proceeding, the bespectacled, antiseptic appearing presiding judge pronounced the sense of the court.

"The murder of Theo van Gogh provoked a wave of revulsion and disdain in the Netherlands. Theo van Gogh was mercilessly slaughtered."

The lack of any real conviction in the judge's tone made one think that he might as well as have been dictating a take-out order for dinner. The hyper-attenuated court atmosphere complete with bomb-sniffing dogs but only a handful of observers, assumed at times a parody.

Making a cultural statement far larger than might have been obvious at the time, at one point during testimony a demand was made for state funded compensation for the "mental anguish" supposedly suffered by two of Holland's feminized policemen. While on the witness stand these two admitted that they had hidden in terror on the floor of their squad car during the final shootout which resulted in the defendant being apprehended.

Bouyeri was convicted on July 26, 2005 and sentenced to life in prison. Holland having long ago abolished the death penalty, ultimate justice was denied, something which under any other circumstance surely would have surely been grist for a van Gogh tirade.

Though the film maker's journey was so ingloriously shortened, he wasn't the only one in transit that morning; the Netherlands and in a larger sense all of Europe was trailing behind him, drawn along figuratively in his wake - a retinue.

The United States was in motion too, it was a day of decision, the quadrennial presidential election - the first national election since the September, 2001 terrorist attacks on New York and Washington, DC.

The contest had already been dismissed, derisively and superficially prejudged by continental media outfits such as Holland's Telegraaf which declared it, "a modern-day crusade, with democracy as its sacred mission...with divine providence on America's side," and then darkly intoning "The growing role and influence of faith in the election campaign has been a source of concern."

That "concern" took the form of contempt in the European press, which derived great satisfaction in stereotyping America as "Jesusland," which was now locked in a monumental electoral struggle, the combatants caricatured to varying degrees.

John Kerry; the erudite, French speaking, continental looking candidate, preaching a secular message which included the clear implication - wildly popular in Europe - that America's rough hewn frontier borne lack of sophistication, should become tempered, domesticated.

The thrust of the critique being that America should emulate Europe or at least move a great deal in that direction.

Germany's Financial Times could hardly conceal its admiration for the Democrat challenger:

> "His first cousin is a French mayor. His father was a diplomat. He spent school years in Switzerland, among other countries, and now and then vacationed in Brittany. His wife grew up in a Portuguese-controlled part of Africa. He thinks the death-penalty is bad and thinks the Kyoto Protocol, intended to protect the global climate, is good. If the Europeans were allowed to vote for the US President this coming November, a triumph for the Democratic challenger John Kerry would be assured..."

Pitted against him, was George Bush; obtusely portrayed as an antagonistic misanthrope. They fancied him a cowboy - Bible thumping and barely literate - despite his Harvard MBA. In their minds Bush was an attack dog, kept, for everyone's sake, on a short leash, only controllable by Dick Cheney and assorted handlers.

[pregnant pause...]

...now he was loose and on a tear in the Middle East...

Britain's Guardian portrayed him as a Christian fanatic invoking the wrath of an angry Deity - "God told me to end the tyranny in Iraq."

There was less philosophical space between the Guardian's

caricature of a born-again soldier of Christ and that of van Gogh than one might have imagined because though the film maker was sublimely dismissive of religion, he was in no way similarly disposed towards faith itself.

Faith drove him - absolute assuredness of purpose is what sped him along every morning or forced him to speak out as he had been doing regarding the cultural upheaval that had accompanied the Muslim defilement of Holland.

> "The Amsterdam police have no interest in coming to the defense of the native Dutch who are being attacked by an increasingly aggressive minority. And [mayor] Cohen couldn't care less. I suspect that our mayor is an incorrigible cynic and a mercenary opportunist to boot, and ask myself for how long the Dutch will be welcome in Amsterdam." - "Our Mayor," Theo van Gogh

But Holland was changing faster than even Europe's most ardent insurrectionists dared hope. This was doubly pleasing because they understood that their stark vision would bleed outwards towards America. The cultural mavens knew that the Netherland's debauched permissivism was to Europe as Europe is the West, the flow inexorably proceeding towards the same fate, separated only by the thinnest slice of time.

CHAPTER THREE - SPIRITUALIZED AND BLINDING IDEOLOGIES...STRANGE GODS

A Controversial Preface:

Two-and-a-half millennia ago Plato [a student of Socrates, generally credited as the father of Western political philosophy] advanced - from the cradle of the Greek democracy, Athens, the idea that engaging in a particular type of discourse - a dialectic, a lively verbal give-and-take between opposing viewpoints would reveal, or at least edge one towards the "truth" or that which was "good, virtuous and noble" through sheer force of reason.

This is all the more remarkable given that Socrates never put quill to parchment, speaking instead through his brightest students - in this case, Plato.

Concerned about how the ethical life should be lived, he was especially interested in exploring the attributes of various forms of government. Believing that the polis should be led by "philosopher kings," it was hoped that through colliding ideas the most just system of stewardship would emerge and then be used - hopefully - by an enlightened monarch to regulate group human behavior and interaction within the body politic.

This belief in the goodness of designer cultures seems to have also made him history's first utopian, not a criticism, especially within the context of ancient cultures in general or of the Greeks themselves who still widely practiced slavery, engaged in bloody warfare and oversaw, with varying degrees of success, a colonial empire.

The dialectic upon which the Greek scholars of the time relied was open ended and set against a backdrop of polytheism in which their numerous gods were capricious. Though these deities were considered quite real, they weren't particularly oracular in the moral sense - displaying all of the frailties of humankind, despite their godlike ability to affect destiny.

We should clarify at this point that the Platonic dialectic differs markedly from the more specialized process upon which Marxism is so heavily reliant. However, because the skeleton of the form is retained in the latter, and since it looms as a central element in that ideology, on the surface it seems to lead one to the reasonable, but false conclusion that Plato served as Marx's progenitor.

While there is certainly an element of paternalistic communalism inherent in Plato's top down micro-management of society, it happens absent Marx's idea of class warfare - a proletarian [in modern times, generally non-white collar, wage-earning] mass of workers who have been defrauded out of the true value of their labor by the power of capital.

Indeed, the concept as Marx imagined it, would have been so bizarre as to be incomprehensible within that society. Additionally, Plato was not advancing a predictive theory of history nor was he philosophizing about an economic system.

To further distinguish between the two, observe that the Marxist notion of the dialectic gains its meaning as used in an adjectival sense "dialectical," a mission specific revision, as a modifier to the nominative "materialism," which limits the scope of inquiry as to remove any recourse in the process to the world of metaphysics.

This is a logical imperative in that absent that qualifier, in open debate one could be lead down the path to self-contradiction, thus neutralizing an essential Marxist tool.

Perhaps more plainly stated, dialectical materialism differs from simple dialectics in one important way. It removes the "God factor/God trap" or more generally for that matter, arguing from a position based upon a moral authority derived from non-changing truth.

Traditionally, dialectics is a process of reasoning which entails pitting varying points of view against each other to produce a synthesis, which should according to the theory, be one step closer to some form of agreed upon truth as seen through Platonic eyes.

Plato's usage implies the presupposition that truth is a definitive quality of existence, something empirically substantial and verifiable within the best capabilities of man. It can also be revealed religious truth, both of which Marxism rejects.

Believers of the "Hammer and Cycle" approach are the ultimate ideologues, knowing in advance where they want their arguments to take them, and so it stands to reason that contrary ideas - which, because of the nature of their origin, are incontestable - must be jettisoned.

Revealed truth is an especially knotty problem for Marxism because it could pit that which has been ordained as being "good," against evil concepts which in a pure dialectical setting produces disaster. How does one compromise with the wicked...just how much of "Hell" is one willing to accept to gain "Heaven?"

No, that math just doesn't work.

It is for this same reason that the left is in reality extraordinarily hostile to knowledge and truth in all forms, not just the religious variety, since both are antithetical to the logic and tools of control. In the Marxist context, truth is always relative, situational and entirely corruptible, the handmaiden of the belief system.

Ideologues are all about the end-game.

Since the time of the "ancient wise ones," rationalism, the empirical method and mankind's considerable intellectual faculties have been used to explore every avenue of human thought, a byproduct of which has been the development of innumerable theories of control [most of which are cleverly disguised] that seek adherence based solely upon the logic of the argument being advanced.

On a practical level, for some two hundred years these systems have been integrated within an archaic, bipolar spectrum: "left" and "right." This usage harkens back to the French Revolution, where those who wished to preserve the crown sat on the right side of the assembly with the revolutionaries taking the opposite side of the room.

Though a tidy arrangement for pointless digressions, in real-time it doesn't work out all that well - the authentic construct of truth is not served. According to the right/left dichotomy, communism is the antipode of fascism. In practice - though theoretically divergent, they're totalitarian brother ideologies.

While both operate under the thumb of a supremely powerful centralized authority, fascism - State Socialism - is a bit more friendly to a limited but crony type capitalism as well as being imbued with a race-conscious ultra-nationalism. As to the latter, Mussolini's racialism looks positively benign compared to Hitler's psychotic hatred and eventual extermination of Jews, gypsies, homosexuals, "social deviants" as well as the physically and mentally handicapped.

Marxists believe that capitalism contains fatal internal contradictions - so flawed that it inherently generates the seeds of its own destruction. Theoretically, Marxism is a deterministic, predictive, historically driven economic hypothesis wherein the privately owned means of production eventually becomes appropriated - through class "struggle" - by the centralized government. In stark reality, most of the relevant private property will have been stolen from individuals by the state, though doctrinally, all the goodies are supposedly being held in common for "the people," in a trust of sorts. This political alignment then equates to the "end of history" - the "dictatorship of the proletariat," with the state then mysteriously, "withering away."

Though it has become the rule to carefully adjust political philosophies [by simplifying and overlooking many of their key elements] to fit within the right/left framework, the appearance of order and correspondence is transitory.

Though the taxonomy sounds manageable, in the most fundamental of ways it's a system based upon a falsely ordered matrix. In action these minutely planned schemes are eerily similar, primarily functioning as chaff for the ever-present iron hand of people who have the means, ability, personality, desire and/or need to control others. To them, ideology is merely an excuse or cover to justify their fetish for ultimate power.

Such is the nature of these self-affirming systems of political thought that the shock troops of such movements often believe in them to the depths of their souls, though of course many would deny the existence thereof.

Taken as a class then these competing philosophies - far from being noble theories of liberation - are instead quite pedestrian jumbles of post-hoc justification. But that isn't their only function; they're the rhetorical equivalent of fog served up as an official cover story which is then dutifully gobbled up and disseminated by the petite bourgeois apparatchiks, the highest level of managers which still contain some true believers.

In an organizational chart these operatives would be just one level below those who smugly push the buttons.

Not wanting to get too far ahead of ourselves or [perish the thought] stray too far, let's just say that the way in which humans make choices works on a multiplicity of levels. Some functions are, metaphorically very close to the surface...we burn our hand on a stove and quickly learn not to repeat such behavior. Others lie quite deep within the mind, at the level of instinct or hunches. Birds build nests and many migrate to warmer climes in the winter...lizards soak up the sun, but they don't know why. Fish spend their entire lives in water, but aren't aware of its presence.

In many ways, political ideologies are limbic in nature, seeping out of that part of the human brain [using the ideas of evolutionary biology as a means to further understand why people do and think the way they do] which is more emotional and primitive.

For the most part then, ideology should be seen as an effort [within the neo-cortex..."human" part of the brain] to offer up or devise a rational grand world-view/justification, an after the fact defense really of feelings, impulses and predispositions which lie buried at a deeper level in the psyche.

Upon endless repetition, sometimes accompanied by various forms and levels of intimidation, and yes, even nurture, the behavior they engender bypasses the circuitry of the rational mind which more closely links cause and effect. For example, a voter pulling the lever for any candidate that happens to have a "D" next to their name on the ballot.

This often takes place despite direct and negative personal experience, such as having seen the last of a city's heavy industrial plants shut down due to an EPA lawsuit initiated by the same party organization to which this voter seems psychically bound.

It's not happenstance that the "rust belt" became so under successive local Democrat administrations, many of which have been run - top to bottom - by African Americans - so it's certainly not attributable to "racism."

For example, Detroit has become a blighted and burned out shell of what used to be the big-shouldered powerhouse of American automobile and related technologies. By some estimates there are now over 30,000 empty homes, and nearly 100,000 vacant lots; some areas lack even basic utilities. The streets are pockmarked, sidewalks are cracked, littered with broken glass and the police are nowhere to be found - yet the dwindling citizenry has been pulling the Democrat lever without fail since 1962.

In one sense this type of behavior can be explained more simply as conditioning, the pigeon pecks the red square and gets a grain of rice; neat and tidy.

Despite the rational side of our nature, all too many will march towards the precipice under color of authority, party banner, ideology or religion, oblivious to the process which draws them towards certain destruction. Though humans aren't lemmings, they can display some of the same behavioral characteristics, resisting arguments which would require them to do things which would force them out of deeply ingrained comfort zones.

Though a man of the left might point to this or that feature of his ideology as justifying his feeling that "the system" unfairly distributes goods and services causing inequality of wealth, often times he will be reacting almost instinctually to an inner conception of fairness which is more a feeling than the result of an entirely rational thought process.

"I feel your pain..."

If one is raised in an environment which reinforces such beliefs, chances are they will carry over into adulthood, barring some transcendent event. The saying that a conservative is a liberal who has been mugged contains more than a bit of truth in that regard.

This doesn't mean that understanding complex political theories and their operative qualities is of no value. It's is a deadly serious business, but the caveat remains; fanaticism is a darkly powerful force - and when confronting one's opponents it's vital to be able, at least at a functional level, be able to speak their language.

In some very large sense these swirling, oft times maddeningly dense, theories serve an unusual role, keeping the rational discussion comfortably at arm's length, providing the antagonists with at least one level of separation [a firewall] from the real issue...who calls the shots. Nonetheless, it's necessary in the arena of ideas to engage with great facility in this three dimensional game of chess if only to retain a sense of credibility within the spirit of academic condescension which is part and parcel of the intellectual battlespace.

As social psychologist Jonathan Haidt cleverly puts it [The Righteous Mind] the model whereby mankind interacts with and "manages" political ideology can be likened to the rider [the rational mind which thinks it's in control] on the back of the hulking elephant [the direction that the evolutionarily adapted, summed inertia of what our natural impulse or inclinations dictate] wherein the animal's pathway can be "nudged" to one side or the other but overridden only with great difficulty. At a deeper level there becomes somewhat of a symbiosis, where the elephant senses the rider's guidance and naturally veers [within certain parameters]in that direction.

Thus political beliefs have much in common with those of a religious nature - though the former can never offer the grand and majestic vision of actually becoming one with the Almighty's creation because of a well-lived life.

One might be born into a religion, a "cradle" Catholic for example and because of this early deep conditioning and immersion into the dogma and its iconography - spoon fed of course in portions which increase as the individual develops the capacity to understand greater nuance and complexity - the likelihood of someone using rational argument to modify or change this body of beliefs is minimal. It generally can only take place internally, perhaps from perceptions caused by a sudden crisis or dramatic revelation which, again, largely bypasses the rational mind.

To put it less adroitly, and of course with all respect due the discipline, as Robert G. Brown, a waggish theoretical physicist at Duke University succinctly states, drawing from the work of David Hume, Philosophy is Bullshit.

In 1739 David Hume wrote, A Treatise on Being, which has great application in the ideas discussed in this chapter.

"All the perceptions of the human mind resolve themselves into two distinct kinds, which I shall call Impressions and Ideas. The difference betwixt these consists in the degrees of force and liveliness with which they strike upon the mind, and make their way into our thought or consciousness. Those perceptions, which enter with most force and violence, we may name impressions; and under this name I comprehend all our sensations, passions and emotions, as they make their first appearance in the soul. By ideas I mean the faint images of these in thinking and reasoning; such as, for instance, are all the perceptions excited by the present discourse, excepting only, those which arise from the sight and touch, and excepting the immediate pleasure or uneasiness it may occasion."

Hume is drawing the distinction between the rational and that which is emotional, instinctual or viscerally felt.

Science is the idyllic purview of the rational, aside from getting emotionally attached to a theory, something which might certainly happen in the case of the theory's author. The complex processes which encompass reasoning are more or less open to change. Realizing that a simple mistake in arithmetic has been made is more than sufficient to absolutely convince most everyone that their checking account balance is, for example, $10.00 more than originally calculated. Perhaps key to this is that there is little of the personal attached to the outcome, aside from the dismissible vanity in admitting that one's mathematical skills may be somewhat lacking.

In contrast, the emotional - largely involuntary - response is far more powerful and less subject to being swayed by argumentation or logic.

Things to which we have a "feeling in the gut" type of response about are of this class...and religion inhabits this same world. We might have been raised within a certain faith or had it come knocking on our door, but once given purchase it is not so easily jettisoned. It's not as if one can be argued out of the propositions of Judaism and into those of Christianity or Buddhism. One simply feels right, there is a sense of inner accord and the other, though it might be held in high esteem or admiration, simply has no resonance within the soul. This is why fallen believers more than occasionally still feel a certain tug of kinship with the family and will take offense when their former faith is treated with less than respect.

Family members might be estranged from each other but woe to the outsider who is foolish enough to meddle.

On an operative level, control is always the imperative which drives these things, not the logic/illogic of the philosophy. If the enemies of society deem that their ideas will have greater impact in a feminized nation, they work to manipulate the ideological climate to bring that about.

...Unsettled yet?

Excellent...

But is it all a sham, some pointless hollowed out game?

Let us assure you, it is not...please be ye not troubled...read on...

Nearly a generation separates us from that chilly, austere morning in 2001 that few Americans will ever forget; but still we stand frozen, immobile, guts boiling...the disease progresses unchecked.

The events of that and subsequent days have led us into believing that keeping America secure - now that the Soviet Union is dead and buried - is essentially a one dimensional undertaking, protecting it from the terrorism of jihadist groups such as al-Qaeda or ISIS.

Though intuitive, coming to the table with preconceptions, thinking in simplified military terms of force and counterforce, deterrence and pro-active or preemptive defense is dangerous...very.

This is no mere jackal biting at our ankles; the universe of threats is hardly limited to organizations or movements which wage kinetic, irregular warfare against the Western democracies. The zone of conflict is clogged with aggressors; enemies both foreign and domestic and they are as resourceful as any foe in the history of warfare. Fully realizing that they would be overmatched in a direct, military confrontation with Uncle Sam or for that matter Britain's John Bull, those who seek to destroy us have adopted a strategy which has, to a greater degree than many realize, already proven successful.

"A nation can survive its fools, and even the ambitious. But it cannot survive treason from within...the traitor moves amongst those within the gate freely, his sly whispers rustling through all the alleys, heard in the very halls of government itself. For the traitor appears not a traitor; he speaks in accents familiar to his victims, and he wears their face and their arguments...He rots the soul of a nation." - Cicero

The most important question at this point in the history of the free world is elemental, but also the one most often left unasked because it's too emotionally wrought; just how secure is the institution we call Western Civilization [in its myriad dimensions] itself?

Understanding the gravity of the issue, our analysis begins tangentially, with one of the most consequential [though little known] legal cases of this era, the landmark federal terror prosecution, "United States of America v. Holy Land Foundation For Relief And Development, et al," Case No. 3:04-CR-240-G, November 30, 2005. Also see 2004 DOJ announcement Holy Land Foundation Leaders, Accused of Providing Material Aid and Support to Hamas Terrorist Organization.

It was a long and complex undertaking, uncovering the funding structure established in the United States which channeled at least $12 million directly to the "Palestinian" terrorist group, HAMAS. After being unable to render a verdict in the first trial, a streamlined case was prepared for the second prosecution. The result of which found all of the defendants guilty on a combined total of 108 charges. Of note, one of those convicted was Ghassan Elashi. Elashi had helped found the Texas chapter of the Council on American Islamic Relations and was already serving a long prison term, having been convicted in another terror-related case, U.S. v. InfoCom, when the Holy Land decision was handed down.

The sheer volume of evidence submitted by the government at trial was overwhelming to the point of being intimidating, but for terror researchers and national security professionals it was a treasure trove of critical new information. For the first time it became possible to understand the dimensions of a paradigm shifting new aspect of the game, a process whereby the jihad could be carried on without a shot being fired.

Two exhibits in particular, showed how all-encompassing this strategy is and the frankly shocking number of domestic Muslim Brotherhood/HAMAS linked organizations that are involved in an effort to subvert the United States.

The first of these was a government filing [see, List of Unindicted Co-conspirators and/or Joint Venturers, PipeLineNews.org] naming dozens of these terror friendly domestic Muslim groups, including the Council on American Islamic Relations [CAIR], the Islamic Society of North America [ISNA] and the North American Islamic Trust [NAIT], an Islamic *waqf* [Arabic for trust or holding company] which owns the deed to many radical American mosques.

Note: both CAIR and ISNA are considered valuable partners by the Obama White House despite their odious connection to the Muslim Brotherhood/HAMAS. Please refer to Steve Emerson and John Rossomando, A Red Carpet for Radicals at the White House, Investigative Project on Terrorism.

In post prosecution actions following the convictions in U.S. v. Holy Land, these organizations were specifically linked to HAMAS by United States District Court [Northern District of Texas] judge Jorge Solis, in an opinion which read in part:

> "The government has produced ample evidence to establish the associations of CAIR, ISNA, NAIT, with NAIT, the Islamic Association for Palestine, and with Hamas," U.S. District Court Judge Jorge Solis said in the July 1, 2009, ruling." [source, The Investigative Project, Federal Dist. Court filing]

The second exhibit is a seminal document, seized in a 2004 terror raid in Virginia. It was written in 1987 but not published until sometime during 1991. Until the Holy Land trial, at best only a handful of people were even aware of its existence, it being part of 80 file boxes of documents which had largely been unexamined. This manifesto was authored by a member of the Muslim Brotherhood, Mohamed Akram. According to Discover the Networks, it was discovered in the home, "of Ismael Elbarasse, a founder of the Dar Al-Hijrah mosque in Falls Church, Virginia."

The plan outlined a detailed blueprint whereby American culture could be targeted by turning every facet of the modern democratic state against itself. This formed the basis for the Brotherhood's long-range game plan of subverting the West. [view Government Exhibit GX3-85, The General Strategic Plan for the Group in North America]. For an interesting perspective on this matter please refer to, Janet Levy, Shielding the Enemy, Family Security Matters.

Thus a new term entered the national security vocabulary, "*civilization jihad,*" a "pre-violent" attack directed at the foundations of the American republic.

Quoting from the Muslim Brotherhood's plan:

> "The process of settlement is a "Civilization-Jihadist Process" with all the word means. The Ikhwan must understand that their work in America is a kind of grand Jihad in eliminating and destroying the Western civilization from within and "sabotaging" its miserable house by their own hand..." [p. 7]

This strategic plan wasn't a new creation, rather it was a clarification of sorts of a similar set of ideas put forth by the Brotherhood and adopted by the Shura Council, the organization's ruling judicial authority, in 1987.

At that time it was clear that the end point which they were working towards was to re-establish the caliphate [a term now in popular sage with the advent of ISIS] globally:

"Enablement of Islam in North America, meaning: establishing an effective and a stable Islamic Movement led by the Muslim Brotherhood which adopts Muslims' causes domestically and globally, and which works to expand the observant Muslim base, aims at unifying and directing Muslims' efforts, presents Islam as a civilizational alternative, and supports the global Islamic State wherever it is." [p. 18]

In this road map, the Brotherhood is urging its followers to mentally make a "fundamental shift" in approach: to become much more aggressive moving from, "a mentality of caution and reservation to "one of risk and controlled liberation" - from a reactive policy to one of being pro-active, "anticipation mentality to initiative mentality" - by abandoning half measures and moving toward "decisiveness" instead of "hesitation."

The Ikhwan urged its directorate and allied organizations to become the leaders of a united front, "the pioneers," allying with other Islamist organizations, "what we reached with the brothers in ICNA [Islamic Circle of North America] "is considered a step in the right direction." [collectively p. 3-4]

Of great importance, they stressed, was to have forward operating bases which will serve as places of congregation, education and action. To this vital role the Brotherhood looks to...the mosque:

"Understanding the role and the nature of work of the Islamic Center in every city with what achieves the goal of the process of settlement: The center we seek is the one which constitutes the axis of our Movement, the perimeter of the circles of our work, our balance center, the base for our rise and our Dar al-Arqam [the base of all operations, a concept going back to time of Mohammed] to educate us, prepare us and supply our battalions in addition to being the niche of our prayers."

And:

"The center ought to turn into a beehive which produces sweet honey…Meaning that the center's role should be the same as the mosque's role during the time of God's prophet…And this was done by…Imam martyr Hasan al-Bana [Egyptian scholar and founder of the Brotherhood] when he and his brothers felt the need to re-establish Islam and its movement anew, leading him to establish organizations with all of their kinds: economic, social, media, scouting, professional and even military ones." [p. 10-11]

Note the militaristic nature of how mosques should ideally function within the Brotherhood's model, equating the activist Muslims to "battalions," truly encompassing the notion of a civilizational jihad with a more than implied reference to physical violence. In "upping the ante," that militancy becomes the watchword, a notion that has grown logarithmically since 9/11.

Though woven throughout a fabric which might superficially invoke religious symbolism, doesn't the substance of the foregoing more closely resemble the language of military commanders as they prepare to engage an enemy or politicians strategizing how to defeat an opponent?

Isn't this really just the lexicon of establishing ideological hegemony?

We will return to these ideas as this essay develops…

Cultures are dynamic structures. At one level they're comprised of individuals, the majority of whom share the same beliefs, customs, language, traditions, legal sensibilities and ethical standards etc. In a more all-encompassing sense civilizations are often an amalgam of cultures which likewise have similar attributes. For example though the French have a culture distinct from that of Britain or of the United States, there is such commonality as to basic purpose and historical experience that they are conjoined, unitized as it were, as members of Western Civilization.

As these attributes change over time, so does the culture. Left to develop on their own, cultures and hence civilizations evolve in a process which is largely organic, i.e., change is [often unconsciously] weighed against tradition, which has already been proven successful. It's the antithesis of the utopian model which creates philosophical blueprints designed to produce the "perfect society" and then seeks to impose them on the status quo, regardless of merit or practicality.

> "One of the dominant ideas which has governed thinking since the 18th century is the idea that we can make everything to our pleasure. That we can design social institutions in their working is basically mistaken. Social institutions have never been designed...They have grown up by a process of selection of the successful without frequently knowing why it was successful. The market is an instrument which enables us to utilize knowledge which is distributed among hundreds of thousands of people. It's an adaptation to thousands of circumstances which nobody can ever know as a whole, where the prices formed on the market tell the individual what to do and what not to do in the social interest..." [source, partial transcript, FA Hayek on Social Justice, Firing Line]

One is reminded here of the aphorism that a camel is a horse designed by committee.

The twentieth century writer and philosopher, G.K. Chesterton understood the value of, and had great appreciation, for ancestral wisdom and the process whereby it is passed from one generation to the next, what Robert Hutchins, then president of Chicago University, called "the grand conversation."

> "In truth, of course, tradition is the most democratic of all things, for tradition is merely a democracy of the dead as well as the living." [source, The Collected Works of G.K.

Chesterton: Chesterton on Dickens, p. 310, St. Ignatius Press]

Preserving the best of what constitutes our heritage, while still allowing for a wary sense of remediation is the heart of political conservatism, a set of ideas which was rekindled in the United States during the post-war 1940s, championed by intellectuals such as the aforementioned Hutchins as well as Christopher Dawson, Russell Kirk, William F. Buckley and others.

There is general agreement that modern conservatism's ideals can be traced back to a European politician who cut a wide swath during the time of the American Revolution, Edmund Burke [1729-1797].

"Burke looked at public issues with almost matchless penetration. Among observers of modern politics only Tocqueville and perhaps Churchill are his rivals in seeing the meaning of events...Burke was discovered for American conservatism as the proponent of a theory of natural law. He was brought forward to oppose the irreligion and relativism of liberals and to provide conservatives with a theory that conceded the political advantages or necessity of religion and the bearing of circumstances on morality, but that nonetheless affirmed natural law, the will of God, as authoritative for men.." [source, History of Political Philosophy, edited by Leo Strauss and Joseph Cropsey, p. 686-689]

Burke was an Irish born political philosopher and long time Member of the House of Commons. While supportive of the American cause, he was above all, a thoughtful man and searched for a means to reconcile the great differences between Britain and the Colonies short of war. He approached the matter practically, suggesting concessions to allow the Colonists to enjoy their freedom without breaking from the orbit of Mother England, thus preserving the established pattern of historical relationships - tradition.

But with tensions on both sides of the Atlantic mounting he came to realize that such measures were probably already too late given the advanced state of decay in affairs. Though it obviously pained him see where events were leading, that didn't stop Burke from declaring that the colonists had the right, as Englishmen, to determine their own future:

> "For, in order to prove that the Americans have no right to their liberties, we are every day endeavouring to subvert the maxims which preserve the whole spirit of our own. To prove that the Americans ought not to be free, we are obliged to depreciate the value of freedom itself; and we never seem to gain a paltry advantage over them in debate, without attacking some of those principles, or deriding some of those feelings, for which our ancestors have shed their blood. [source, Edmund Burke, <u>Speech Regarding Conciliation with the Colonies</u>, March 22, 1775]

Or as James Madison wrote in Federalist 51:

> "But what is government itself, but the greatest of all reflections on human nature? If men were angels, no government would be necessary. If angels were to govern men, neither external nor internal controls on government would be necessary. In framing a government which is to be administered by men over men, the great difficulty lies in this: you must first enable the government to control the governed; and in the next place oblige it to control itself."

Burke was also quick to illustrate the relationship between freedom and self-restraint, the essence of conservatism:

> "Men are qualified for civil liberty in exact proportion to their disposition to put moral chains upon their own appetites."

As always, the MP's counseled against radical change, which was reflected in his laissez-faire attitude towards British dealings with the Colonies:

"Grenville [George Grenville, Prime Minister] wasn't anything if not conscientious. He was said to be the first British minister who actually read the colonial dispatches. His ill-fated attempts to impose fiscal discipline on the colonies prompted the first serious, continent-wide resistance to royal authority. Grenville had ended the policy of a century-and-a-half of what the great parliamentarian Edmund Burke would call, "a wise and salutary neglect." [source, William J. Bennett, America - The Last Best Hope, Vol I, p. 67]

Contrasted against the American cause, Burke saw everything that was wrong with utopianism reflected in the French Revolution, the blood-lust and envy which defined it and the Jacobins, the revolution's Waffen SS, which oversaw and enforced its reign of terror.

The British legislator - a particularly gifted orator - railed against the radical ideologies of his day, believing instead in slow, thoughtful, evolutionary change, i.e., caution of action based upon a respect for previous experience because it relied on ideas and methods which had survived the test of time.

Of note, the Burkean approach to a changing world has wide applicability in matters as diverse as the philosophy of law:

> "The emphasis on incrementalism and gradualism evokes the philosophy of Edmund Burke, who viewed governance as a practical endeavor guided by experience grounded in skepticism of grand political theories. Burke counseled deference to long-settled practices and traditions tested by experience and the collective wisdom of society accumulated over generations. He held the common law in high regard..." [source, Originalism v. Minimalism, CATO Institute]

Three concepts figured large within his political calculus, "prejudice," by which he meant consciously making choices based upon prior experience, "presumption," accepting that the past often points the way forward and "prescription," the application of this sometimes ancient wisdom as an ameliorating force in dealing with societal problems.

There was another reason - implicit - in Burke's defense of tradition. It serves to foster long term social stability, knitting the generations together by making it possible to pass along shared historical experience and custom from the older to the younger. As we will see later, failure to attend to this process can lead to unsustainable, discontinuous societies where the young have so little in common that they might as well inhabit a different planet.

> "Edmund Burke's political theory was engendered in the context of the unfolding drama of modernity. In particular, his political ideas were a response to the rise of radical ideologies like Jacobinism. *But the circumstances of the eighteenth century may have been worse than Burke surmised...*" [emphasis added, source, Michael P. Federici, The Politics of Prescription: Kirk's Fifth Canon of Conservative Thought , First Principles]

This reference was a caveat which Burke hadn't considered, at least as reflected in his writings.

Imagine a political ideology held with canonical fervor. What if, as it was then and increasingly has been the case over the last 100 years to many in the intellectual class, the religious concept of "truth" no longer has meaning?

In that case belief systems can easily be put to service in the resultant religious vacuum which is ready-made to be filled by a secular, theistic-like ideology:

> "...Irving Babbitt recognized by the early twentieth century that Burke had underestimated the spiritual strength of radical ideologies bent on uprooting traditional ideas and the prescriptive institutions of Western Civilization. Burke dismissed the radicals of the

eighteenth century as "half a dozen grasshoppers...with their importunate chink." The men of tradition he compared to "thousands of great cattle, reposed beneath the shadow of the British oak." Although they are silent, they outnumber and outweigh in character the "little, shriveled, meager, hopping, though loud and troublesome, insects of the hour." Babbitt, however, replies that "the little, meager, hopping insects of the hour were representatives of an international movement of a vast scope, a movement destined finally to prevail over the prejudice and prescription that Burke was defending." [source, *ibid*]

The utopian's dictates aren't intended to be interpreted but rather adhered to with a dogmatic fundamentalism. These beliefs are impervious to argumentation because they are agents of control founded upon invented imperatives; within the leftist framework, the old order must [and deserves to] be overturned. So, for example one might be encouraged to be a sexual libertine or to support the confiscation of all civilian firearms as being just, however merely criticizing a subversive Black president or drawing cartoons of a half-mad prophet makes one a hater - these days a serious social crime.

There is no appeal to such a charge and worse, ironically being so classified becomes sufficient justification for a level of genuine hatred so great that violence becomes countenanced as the "moral" response.

"Kill the haters..."

Classical, religiously derived [Judeo-Christian] ethical road-maps which have been tested and either accepted in full, in part or totally rejected depending on their efficacy, fundamentally differ from the "moral" dictates of the puppet masters. The later establish non-negotiable, intransigent behavioral baselines which fail [among a great many other flaws] to allow for the high probability of - and since it is human nature to which we are referring - being wrong.

Social architects encourage intellectual intimidation, civil unrest, acts of violence, armed repression or even warfare based upon simple-minded declaratives and slogans such as "Black Lives Matter" [and the ethnic strife which it has already brought forth] or that "the religion of God and His Prophet, Mohammed" must not be denigrated or insulted.

Societies governed under such regimes are de-facto police states, even absent checkpoints and razor-wire barriers.

Within the Western notion of modernity even the fervency of that which appears to be religiously absolute, the 8th Commandment, "Thou Shalt Not Steal," for example, requires some level of context in order to be considered justly applicable.

So does moral confusion reign supreme, is it a major breach of the eighth Commandment to steal a loaf of bread to feed a starving child?

Technically/literally, of course, but there are mitigating circumstances, since it's more than reasonable to assume that most Western theologians would argue that there is greater good in keeping an innocent alive rather than cowering in absolute fidelity to an inflexible law that could do great harm. This can be persuasively argued because one cannot be absolved from moral responsibility by hiding behind even such long standing precedents as the Ten Commandments.

Furthermore, in any context, stealing a loaf of bread is a minor offense and hence, the moral quandary encompassed in the "ends vs. means" dilemma need not apply. This is an important concept since utopians are quite often willing to commit evil [mass murder, suspension of civil rights, etc.] under the rationale that it's being done "for the greater or common good" of society.

In this manner the West's two great religions can positively be reconciled with secular ethics and moral philosophy. To Christians and Jews general guidelines are all well and good but they aren't unyielding. The basis for drawing this conclusion is that since the Almighty has blessed man with a free will as well as the capacity to reason he is expected to sort out the gray areas himself without "further consultation," excepting prayer and reflection for guidance.

This is not the case either with Islam or progressivism/Marxism, which are remarkably similar in that they share an identical ethos - they can't be intellectually validated because their strictures don't abide accommodation, instead relying on mindless compulsion. Under the Shari'a, the prescription for theft is cutting off of the hand, likewise, the Marxist solution for "unearned" wealth is confiscation. The former appeals to the Qur'an and Hadith, the latter finds justification within the hypotheses of a mid 19th century political philosopher, though at a base level it is really driven by human greed and envy.

Theories so derived are inherently dangerous in usage, having acquired, via the assertion of the ground-breaking, sheer intellectual brilliance of their author[s], moral authority.

Because of the fervor with which they are held they're entirely inflexible and demand total fealty by believer and non-believer alike - despite being entirely secular.

"Why is that illegal?"

"Because I say so."

The 19th century philosopher Hilaire Belloc put forth a novel line concerning Islam, arguing that rather than being a genuine and unique religion, it was really an heretical distortion of Catholicism, appropriated by Mohammed, and pruned down to size for easy consumption among the nomadic Bedouin tribes.

> Mohammedanism was a <heresy>: that is the essential point to grasp before going any further. It began as a heresy, not as a new religion...o[but as] a perversion of Christian doctrine. It vitality and endurance soon gave it

the appearance of a new religion, but those who were contemporary with its rise saw it for what it was-not a denial, but an adaptation and a misuse, of the Christian thing...[the heresiarch] sprang from pagans. But that which he taught was in the main Catholic doctrine, oversimplified

He took over very few of those old pagan ideas which might have been native to him from his descent. On the contrary, he preached and insisted upon a whole group of ideas which were peculiar to the Catholic Church and distinguished it from the paganism...the unity and omnipotence of God. The attributes of God he also took over in the main from Catholic doctrine: the personal nature, the all-goodness, the timelessness, the providence of God, His creative power as the origin of all things, and His sustenance of all things by His power alone. The world of good spirits and angels and of evil spirits in rebellion against God was a part of the teaching, with a chief evil spirit, such as Christendom had recognized. Mohammed preached with insistence that prime Catholic doctrine, on the human side-the immortality of the soul and its responsibility for actions in this life, coupled with the consequent doctrine of punishment and reward after death. [source, Hilaire Belloc, The Great Heresies, The Great and Enduring Heresy of Mohammed, p. 36-37]

However Mohammed denied Christ his Godhead, the incarnation, which had the effect of elevating Mohammed several orders of magnitude up the food chain, making him the "final prophet," a role in which he continues to serve among the inheritors of his way of life and commands.

Islamic doctrine is all about power and subjugating believers [who voluntarily "submit"] and non-believers alike. As the 6th president of the United States, John Quincy Adams noted, Islam has nothing of the spiritual about it:

"In the seventh century of the Christian era, a wandering

Arab of the lineage of Hagar, the Egyptian, combining the powers of transcendent genius, with the preternatural energy of a fanatic, and the fraudulent spirit of an impostor, proclaimed himself as a messenger from Heaven, and spread desolation and delusion over an extensive portion of the earth. Adopting from the sublime conception of the Mosaic law, the doctrine of one omnipotent God; he connected indissolubly with it, the audacious falsehood, that he was himself his prophet and apostle. Adopting from the new Revelation of Jesus, the faith and hope of immortal life, and of future retribution, he humbled it to the dust, by adapting all the rewards and sanctions of his religion to the gratification of the sexual passion. He poisoned the sources of human felicity at the fountain, by degrading the condition of the female sex, and the allowance of polygamy; and he declared undistinguishing and exterminating war, as a part of his religion, against all the rest of mankind. THE ESSENCE OF HIS DOCTRINE WAS VIOLENCE AND LUST: TO EXALT THE BRUTAL OVER THE SPIRITUAL PART OF HUMAN NATURE." [Robert Spencer, The Politically Incorrect Guide To Islam And The Crusades p 83, emphasis in the original]

WARNING - Bold Assertion: While Islam is a political force to be reckoned with, despite its large numbers of believers, it's no more a religion than are the ideas expressed in Machiavelli's, The Prince. Actually Machiavelli's lack of pretense and/or appeal to a certitude based upon celestial truths or revelation imbues his ideas with a sense of the authentic which Islam totally lacks.

During the latter half of the 19th century, the philosopher Friedrich Nietzsche was reflecting on a world which in his view was rapidly becoming estranged from the grandeur and simplicity of previous ages, where man had become suspicious of all that his ancestors held dear:

"God is dead. God remains dead. And we have killed him. How shall we, the murderers of all murderers, comfort ourselves? That which was holiest and mightiest of all that the world has yet possessed has bled to death under our knives - who will wipe this blood off us? With what water could we purify ourselves? What festivals of atonement, what sacred games will we need to invent? Isn't the greatness of this deed too great for us? Must we not ourselves become gods simply to seem worthy of it?" [Friedrich Nietzsche, The Gay Science, Section 125, The Madman]

He saw an emptiness descending on humanity where the only freedom offered was a false promise, a release from the "bondage" of ritual and the duty to do that which is right. He presciently saw in this the probability of a nihilism constrained only loosely by the fickle and expansive concept of moral/ethical relativism, from which he saw little alternative.

"What I relate is the history of the next two centuries. I describe what is coming, what can no longer come differently: the advent of nihilism. For some time now our whole European culture has been moving as toward a catastrophe, with a tortured tension that is growing from decade to decade: restlessly, violently, headlong, like a river that wants to reach the end." [Nietzsche, Will to Power, Preamble, Towards an Outline]

Writing decades before Nietzsche, Karl Marx was by no means off put off by an "artificially" ordered world, entering the scene in 1848 with the publication of the Communist Manifesto - "Let the ruling classes tremble at a Communistic revolution. The proletarians have nothing to lose but their chains. They have a world to win."

Having thus gained considerable visibility, Marx's polemic was followed by what has come to represent the Bible of the left, Das Kapital [1867, volume I], co-authored by Friedrich Engels. In it they proposed a tripartite theory of causation - at once an economic system, a political ideology as well as a deterministic theory of history. Marxism was so all-encompassing it could be understood as having a moral nature in that it served as an ethical indictment of capitalism, a term that he put into common usage. As used in this framework, "capitalism" becomes stigmatized as a pejorative.

At the time nineteenth century Europe was mired in social turmoil, much of it the result of the rapid onset of the Industrial Revolution [especially the impact of steam powered machinery] and the dislocation that it caused. Where in the recent past, Europeans had worked with their hands, aided by the power of draft animals, the mechanization of the workplace represented a genuine paradigmatic change, which mandated a commensurate alteration in the way the populace looked at work. People were fearful and angry over the loss of their previous lifestyle; many were resentful at the very presence of machines in the work place, culminating in riots by "Luddites," bent on smashing these new creations.

In the light of and taking advantage of these developments, Marx's proposition was complex. He predicted that capitalism was unsustainable and that the state would pass through various stages of development, eventually dematerializing, to be replaced by a dictatorship of the proletariat - the oppressed working class.

Having been named and honored as the central player in Marx's theory and destined to eventually lead society, had obvious appeal to the working class. Similarly Marxism had the ability to also draw in those who saw themselves in a leadership role, guiding the proletariat to this Promised Land.

Marx struck with such power that even the Church felt obligated to respond, which Pope Leo XIII, did in 1891 with the supremely ill-considered Encyclical, Rerum Novarum - On Capital and Labor [note, for a more detailed treatment of this subject please refer to this author's monograph, <u>Bitter Harvest: How Marxist "Progressives" Have Infiltrated the American Catholic Church</u>].

This was a grave strategic error on the part of the Pontiff who should never have attempted to craft a Christian based economic refutation of Marxist dogma because doing so only served to give the theory added credibility. Leo looked foolish in what appeared to be a derivative and vague attempt at rebutting that for which he wasn't equipped to understand.

Though Rerum Novarum spans some 14,000 words, socialism is mentioned only 5 times while the caveats, of which there are many, serve to negate whatever effect they might have had, for example:

> "Doubtless, before deciding whether wages are fair, many things have to be considered; but wealthy owners and all masters of labor should be mindful of this - that to exercise pressure upon the indigent and the destitute for the sake of gain, and to gather one's profit out of the need of another, is condemned by all laws, human and divine."

Or

> "...justice demands that, in dealing with the working man, religion and the good of his soul must be kept in mind. Hence, the employer is bound to see that the worker has time for his religious duties; that he be not exposed to corrupting influences and dangerous occasions; and that he be not led away to neglect his home and family, or to squander his earnings."

Such statements make neither economic sense nor are they rooted in scripture and its clear from the wording that Leo felt that despite the rote requirement of "rejecting" socialism and socialists that there was something very wrong with capitalism.

The effect Rerum Novarum had was profound, reflected in the subsequent publishing of "Distributive Justice, the Right and Wrong of Our Present Distribution of Wealth," authored by Monsignor John Augustine Ryan

About Ryan, the University of St. Thomas website contains the following:

"John Ryan's position as an economist and Catholic leader emerged more strongly after moving back to Washington, DC, and becoming a professor at CUA in 1915. He published another major monograph, Distributive Justice: The Right and Wrong of Our Present Distribution of Wealth, in 1916. Based on his interpretation and understanding of Rerum Novarum and extensive study of several plans for the reconstruction of post war societies Ryan wrote the critically important Bishop's Program of Social Reconstruction, issued by the National Catholic War Council in the name of American Bishops in 1919. The Bishop's Program became the guiding force for the National Catholic Welfare Council's Social Action Department and Catholic progressives in the 1920s and 1930s. Many of the recommendations in the Bishop's Program were enacted 15 years later during Franklin D. Roosevelt's New Deal."

Previous to "Distributive Justice," Ryan had written, "A Programme of Social Reform By Legislation," which was characterized as "a kind of wish list of reform aimed at the worst abuses caused by economic changes..."

Since that point there has been a 100 year process during which the Catholic Church has been taken over by Marxist theologians masquerading as social justice warriors and this abrupt turning away from the Church's primary role in saving souls is reflected in a wholesale emptying of the pews.

From the foregoing it's impossible not to conclude that the Church's thinking on these matters has undergone a complete reversal and it naturally follows therefore that the "enemy" of the faith is no longer Satan or even a mystically defined, but very real "evil." Instead, to the Pope and the ecclesiastical bureaucratic governorate that serves him, the greatest moral threat facing mankind is seen as capitalism, ironically the sole guarantor of the Church's ability to worship - however unwisely - in freedom. While the average Catholic might not be able to explain it to the satisfaction of an academic, they know it when they see it and at this gut level they are entirely correct.

Ayn Rand drew the conflict between these competing Western systems as a duel between altruism and self-interest.

> "Capitalism is in the process of committing suicide and if we want to stop that process we must understand its reasons...no political system in history had proved its value so eloquently or had benefitted mankind so greatly as capitalism.."

> Noting that capitalism has singularly been attacked "so savagely and blindly," Rand tied the unwillingness to challenge Marxism by the establishment to "a primordial evil," the morality of "altruism" the idea that "mankind has no right to exist for its own sake...that service to others is the only justification of his existence." [source, Rand on capitalism, You Tube video]

This leaves us with two major and antagonistic, temporally sacralized systems of belief, the goal of each being the "fundamental transformation" of society, albeit for different but somewhat interrelated purposes.

As used here the agents of transformation are intellectual constructs directed towards the eventual eradication of Western Civilization, which we use in the expansive sense of changing it so radically that it's no longer recognizable. This can be a full frontal assault, as was the case in the French Revolution, or a less direct but possibly more dangerous method of stealthily toppling the foundational elements of democratic, free-market republicanism: liberty [as in individual free choice as opposed to group rights], private property, capitalism and of course the moral imperative which drives the process, the post-Reformational Judeo Christian ethic.

So vital is the concept of a revealed or generally accepted moral philosophy affirming truth [again the Platonic concept of "the good"] that even one of a "deviational" nature, which might be seen more broadly, but still reverentially as a creation myth, might well suffice because it would nonetheless serve as an ethical guidepost originating from a loftier authority than that of man, assuming it had proven itself as worthy and humane over a very long span of time, as has traditional Judeo-Christian, Western morality.

Homo Sapiens are nothing if not quirky and mysterious in some very basic ways. For example humanity has locked within its DNA - perhaps something to do with the fundamental evolutionary mandate required for species survival - a seemingly peculiar mechanism which psychologically grants "permission" for even "good people" to engage in what are normally considered sociopathic or barbaric acts, including doing great violence to others or one's self [dying for a cause] in order to preserve the things which are considered to be so over-archingly essential that they are worth securing at any and all cost.

In that sense consider the horrific Allied fire-bombing of Tokyo during the last six months of World War II. The raids burned at least 100,000 Japanese civilians to death while wounding as many as a million. This was not a war-crime; it was an exigency which was required to destroy the Imperial Japanese - who had initiated hostilities - thus allowing America to survive the bloodiest conflict in history, with an intact culture.

Social psychologists, theologians, etc., have attached a name which serves to objectify the class of intellectual [or physical] constructs which meet this specialized definition, calling them "sacred objects."

Though the term can be used as a jumping off point in pursuit of wild deconstructionist tangents in the intellectual war against the West, the idea neatly encapsulates the degree of devotion which spiritualized ideologies can and do engender. Its function as an identifier aids in our understanding the power which these "strange-gods" have over human behavior, granting them moral authority over that which would [absent context] normally be considered ethically reprehensible.

This is especially true in an environment which has been denuded of traditionalism which, even though itself can be thought of as a collection of sacred objects, is one which has proven by its very existence, not to be self-destructive. This is the reason why understanding the   difference between organically evolved change versus that which is simply imposed is so central to understanding the current cultural drift and the value of maintaining operationally non-hostile ethical/moral systems.

However absent the constraining influence of an ethically delimited tradition, utopian ideologies can quickly morph into license to murder, often on a mass scale.

The implications of this theory have been tested in laboratory settings and proven valid.

Consider the research of social psychologist Stanley Milgram who, at Yale University during the 1960s explored the implications of obedience within a rigid entirely secular hierarchy.

Briefly, Milgram placed two volunteers into a scenario in which one was designated the interlocutor and the other the party being questioned, thus establishing an unequal hierarchical authority relationship:

Milgram => interlocutor => test subject.

The questioner [who was advised that his strict obedience to the protocol would be of "great benefit to science"] was instructed by the researcher to administer a series of supposed electrical shocks to the subject when they answered a question incorrectly.

In actuality, there was no flow of electricity; the party being interrogated was instructed to play along as if he was really being tortured in this manner.

The ground rules held that the pain would continue to increase until the question was correctly answered even upon the understanding that at the highest level the voltage would supposedly be lethal.

In what was clearly surprising to the researcher, 2/3rds of the inquisitors followed orders to the letter and proceeded to administer what they believed to be a fatal jolt to the other party simply upon the understanding of having been given "permission" by an authority figure who claimed to be acting for a higher good, in this case that of science.

This is the basic mechanism whereby the foot soldiers of the progressive left and the Islamists feel ethically unfettered in pursuing their utopian schemes believing that they're "working for the greater or common good" or pursuing "more lofty, even godly" purpose which is, in the case of these two "isms" a prescription for horror.

We have hopefully demonstrated the fundamental error of such thinking but regardless, another complication arises. There is an added dimension to these high order ideologies, that of motivation.

Assume that this segment of the population generally accepts the dogmatic beliefs which are offered in justifying its actions, call them the true believers.

But what about the leaders of these movements, the sparkplugs of the revolution?

Is it surprising to find out that the decision makers often approach their roles in a totally cynical manner? Those who have the personality type consistent with a desire to control people use ideology as merely an excuse or cover to justify their totalitarian bent.

Take the left's most recent cause, that of "transgender equality." Pity those who actually sup at this table, who believe that their vouchsafed ideology logically supports the proposition that it's entirely natural to allow "gender challenged" biological males to shower in the girls locker room, but understand that for every one who asserts this nonsense, there are others, more cynical/realistic who understand it for the game that it is, another aspect of the pathway to dominion, serving to erode the foundation of the dominant culture.

While not dealt with in this section, or the work overall - since it more involves potential solutions to our crisis, rather than being part of the analysis of how we got here - is the weighty question of whether an ideology based upon political conservatism is even relevant to the dire state of Western Civilization, so we wish to briefly acknowledge the issue which will be exhaustively dealt with in the next volume of this series:

Looked upon from a distance so as to gain as much perspective as possible, when viewing the great expanse of the history of the West post the introduction of Marxism-Leninism, we see a culture that would be in many regards almost impossible for a citizen from roughly the first half of the twentieth century to recognize as being American.

Things have changed so substantially that if someone from let's say 1930 was given a glimpse of the future - our current reality - they would of course be amazed and most likely dazzled by the new technologies but if allowed to look a little deeper it is this writer's guess that this "time traveler" would be in equal parts dumbstruck and sickened by the mores [such as they are] which now govern the West.

Now for the conundrum; using the Burkean ideological model [even as updated by the new conservatives such as Buckley, Podhoretz, Irving Kristol and others] the prescriptive strategy would be to halt the process whereby novelty and utopian thinking is being used to supplant traditionalism...2016 frozen in time.

Looked at one way, this of course makes total sense; once the captain of the ship notices it's off course the first step it to halt its bad heading.

But then what?

Say we could simply turn back the clock or use a "restore point" to roll history backwards to the days preceding World War I.

Since the restoration would be global in context, all of the accoutrements which currently make contemporary life so much richer, diverse, more beautiful, easier and less painful would vanish in a flash.

Yes gone would be Black Lives Matter, the 60s revolution, frightening restrictions on the 2nd and 10th Amendments, Johnson's disastrous war as well as his Great Society, but in just a single example, many of the personal freedoms which the majority now take as a birthright would be gone.

Jim Crow would still be in force, there would be no social safety net to help protect the truly needy and most of us would still be toiling long dangerous hours in the agricultural society - or a heavy industry where the personal safety of workers was of little concern - where an early death was almost a given by modern standards, given that in 1930 life expectancy was less than 60 years of age.

Women leaders in the workplace or politics, social "deviants" - anyone who broke the rigid moral code [gays/lesbians/sexual libertines, recreational drug users, hipsters, non-Christians, "edgy" artists/musicians/non-conformists in general...the list goes on nearly forever] would be anathematized and would pay a steep social price.

The truth is that significant numbers of Americans want their online porn, to have the freedom to smoke cannabis, dye their hair purple, make fun of religion and religious people as well as "heathens" and "pagans," amass great quantities of firearms, play "Death Metal" or "Devil music," or to generalize it more broadly, to be as Freud wrote about in his 1929 book, Civilization and its Discontents, rebels and deviants.

Though there are obvious problems associated with such aberrant behavior, properly managed it's difficult to imagine how a classically liberal but modern society, [one in which liberty and freedom are maximized and continuously refreshed] can flourish, absent their existence.

In modeling a contemporary model of the West one must allow its citizens the liberty to live outside the cultural norm as long as the basic moral code upon which the West is founded - your freedom to swing your fist stops at the point of my nose, at its most basic.

Thus if liberty is to remain a living thing, a multiplicity of lifestyles have to be accommodated, but only upon the key proviso [which applies to all under the Western theory of the social contract] that the individual must embrace acculturation, neither become a burden to society nor expect the majority to underwrite perverse, iconoclastic, self-destructive/odd manners of living or force others to live according to the social misfit's [no pejorative intended] "guiding light."

The irony of permitting a great deal of controlled deviance, is that the product thereof often contributes to a richer, more beautiful world, a perfect example of which would be the dissidence which often drives the arts.

Lest one draw the wrong conclusion, this is by no means "multiculturalism;" it's merely allowing for a certain amount of controlled deviation within a long established and thus proven, societal norm and not the acceptance of a society comprised of an amalgam of unrelated [often hostile] entities forever at war with each other.

But traditional conservatism tends towards strongly suppressing aberrant innovation and the fact remains that even if it were possible to reset the culture pre a certain troublesome period, the negative aspects of that particular time in history would inevitably follow.

Taking into full account what we now know [and are about to discover in the following chapters] about the obvious downward spiral which seemingly entraps us - and upon the realization that there is really no going back - a strictly enforced conservatism which would freeze us in place at any point in history would be extraordinarily harmful.

Even allowing for the type of slow natural evolution which Burkean conservatism permits such a move would be as disastrous as is pursuing the present trend. To forcibly halt "progress" in shark filled waters while inexorably drifting towards oblivion [because of the inertia which societal drivers already in place, empower] - a "frozen" culture - therefore can never be the answer, once the damage has already been done.

Because of this we are forced to realize that there is really no point in the past in which it would be wise, even if possible, to park America.

Actually it would be immoral.

Though difficult, perhaps impossible to accept - upon first reading by some, if not many - we assert that conservatism is theoretically/inherently/technically incapable of defeating progressivism because its basic nature is accommodative and it's morally and ethically indefensible to bargain with evil.

If we persist in asserting this proven failure of a doctrine the effect will only be to worsen our current predicament. We will figuratively be sending our soldiers out, against superior forces, across a mine filled "no-man's-land" into the maw of machine gun emplacements, totally unarmed.

So with our once mighty hammer thus gelded what do we do?

As previously alluded to, remedial measures will be dealt with in future writings. Nonetheless we feel that it would be remiss not to raise the issue in the light of the insistence by the old guard to cling to what is an obviously defective conservative banner as it desperately sought to derail the Trump candidacy.

Fact: conservatism was never meant to serve as a salvific force under all conditions.

CHAPTER FOUR - THE UNHOLY ALLIANCE

We turn to a closer examination of the two previously identified hyper-aggressive ideologies, one of which is that of the progressive/neo-Marxists. It is correct to consider the term broadly, so as to include non-classical liberalism and so-called "moderate" leftism because over time, they're functionally identical. Note the morphing of Democrat party over the last century from the conservative, traditional liberalism of president Grover Cleveland [1837-1908] to the statism of Barack Hussein Obama.

It's a downward slope to totalitarian rule towards which political gravity irresistibly draws us ever nearer.

To those who might object, claiming it's an unjustifiably expansive definition, let us offer an analogy. Consider two co-workers at XYZ Inc., going through the daily grind of driving to work. Though one of these people might build muscle cars on the weekends thus minutely understanding the intricacies which make up automobile performance, his counterpart might be challenged with simple tasks such as properly inflating his tires or checking the oil level.

Yet despite these vast differences, both use the same tool, in an identical manner to arrive at the same place. Scratch a liberal and, eventually, collectivist blood will flow: this is manifestly not Jack Kennedy's party and today's "liberals" should more correctly be thought of as gestating Marxists.

The second of these creeds is a unique entity, a politically-driven quasi-religion, Islam, which is defiantly revolutionary. Grounded upon the Shari'a [Islamic religious law] outside of ritual, it's very much about political power, conquest and consequently, dominion.

This has been the case with Islam as it has been normatively practiced since it was conceived in the seventh century, with only brief periods of quiescence. The Shari'a is derived from three sources:

> The Qur'an - understood to be the very word of Allah - as "revealed" to Mohammed, carried by the angel Gabriel. This extraordinary experience took place when Islam's prophet was about 40 years of age, approximately the year 610 AD.

> The Sunnah, the way of the Prophet, an orally transmitted collection of lessons drawn from the life of Mohammed.

> The Hadith, commentary by religious scholars on Islam, the teachings of the Prophet.

Both of these philosophies must be viewed as enemy threat doctrines. In close focus they share many attributes, but when seen from a wider perspective the commonality of features is even greater because in many ways, Marxism is effectively the Shari'a of the left.

As the once mighty Ottoman Empire was crumbling at the end of World War I, the philosophy of Islamic global jihad was already being exhumed and readied for battle in the new age. It was heavily influenced in the 20th century by the work of an Egyptian Muslim Brotherhood theoretician, Seyyid Qutb and that of the Indo-Pakistani writer Abul A'la Mawdudi [Maududi] who quite forthrightly proclaimed Islam to be a revolutionary ideology.

> "In 1926, in a work that anticipates most of the ideological developments of the past two decades, the youthful Mawdudi had declared: "Islam is a revolutionary ideology and a revolutionary practice, which aims at destroying the social order of the world totally and rebuilding it from scratch...and jihad [holy war] denotes the revolutionary struggle." Mawdudi conceived the modern world as the arena of the "conflict between Islam and un-Islam," the later being equated with pre-Islamic ignorance [jahiliyya] and polytheism. Modern creeds and political philosophies

were equated with polytheism and ignorance. Their predominance necessitated the revival of Islam..." [source, Said Amir Arjomand, <u>Revolution, Critical Concepts in Political Science</u>, Rosemary H. T. O'Kane, Ed, p. 296]

Mawdudi considered Islam to be a duality, a mixture of both religion and political ideology:

"Islam is a revolutionary doctrine and system that overturns governments. It seeks to overturn the whole universal social order...and establish its structure anew...Islam seeks the world. It is not satisfied by a piece of land but demands the whole universe...Islamic Jihad is at the same time offensive and defensive...The Islamic party does not hesitate to utilize the means of war to implement its goal." [source, Yvonne Haddad, "Islamists and the Challenge of Pluralism," Washington, D.C.: Center for Contemporary Arab Studies at Georgetown University, 1995, p. 10]

He saw a certain degree of similarity between elements of Marxism [for example the idea of a political "vanguard," i.e., the standard bearers who were expected to advance the movement] and his developing ideas as he worked towards a reformational Islam. These were incorporated into a new fundamentalism, given form in Pakistan's Jamaat-e-Islami, which he created. His impact on the development of the pan-Islamic movement, or modern Islamism has been great and is often overlooked

As evidence of this influence, it was Mawdudi who authored the chapter on "jihad" in a primer on the Muslim religion - Towards Understanding Islam - which is widely distributed at the conferences/conventions of Muslim Brotherhood front groups. In it he says:

"Jihad is a part of this overall defense of Islam...in the language of the Divine Law, this word is used specifically for the war that is waged solely in the name of God against those who perpetrate oppression as enemies of Islam. This supreme sacrifice is the responsibility of all Muslims...jihad is as much a primary duty as are daily prayers or fasting. One who avoids it is a sinner. His every claim to being a Muslim is doubtful. He is plainly a hypocrite who fails in the tests of sincerity and his acts of worship are a sham, a worthless hollow show of devotion..." [source, Abul A'la Mawdudi, "Towards Understanding Islam," p. 124-125]

To understand the principle in its totality, one must parse the above, noting that in Islamic theology, an "enemy" of Islam is anything [including the totality of the Western edifice] which impedes the imposition of "God's religion" globally, a concept which might alternatively be thought of in terms of an offensive defense.

Qutb, whose most influential contributions towards a reconfigured Islam occurred post World War II, also closely identified with the concept of political "vanguardism" - a central core leadership of believers who must separate themselves from 'jahili' society [that of the unbelievers and the "ignorant," which could include Muslims who fell outside his vision of an incendiary philosophy] - to lead humanity toward the "true or purified Islam."

"It is therefore necessary that Islam's theoretical foundation - belief - materialize in the form of an organized and active group from the very beginning. It is necessary that this group separate itself from the jahili society...the center of this new group should be new leadership...which first came in the person of the Prophet: [Milestones, p. 47]

In Marxist nomenclature this would be labeled a "united front."

This studious intellectual was a keen observer. In a sense, the central point of his scathing indictment of the West was as valid then as it is today. Our civilization has been brought to its knees, no longer able to "present healthy values for the guidance of mankind." The irony that one of jihadism's most influential architects [for example, his works, especially Milestones, were a staple in many al-Qaeda and other Sunni jihadist encampments] could so eloquently identify the disease which today plagues us is hard to overlook.

> "Mankind today is on the brink of a precipice, not because of the danger of complete annihilation which is hanging over its head - this being just a symptom and not the real disease - but because humanity is devoid of those vital values which are necessary not only for its healthy development but also for its real progress. Even the Western world realizes that Western civilization is unable to present any healthy values for the guidance of mankind...It is essential for mankind to have a new leadership...Islam is the only system which possesses these values and this way of life. [Milestones, p. 7]

Qutb raises a serious issue here which deserves a much more lengthy treatment; the sybaritic/hedonistic qualities which the West, and we must assume, all industrialized nations have come to acquire. The truth of this element of the larger Islamic ideological attack on modernism should be self-evident.

Once freed from a subsistence way of life, the need to fight every day for basic survival, cultures seem to succumb, to one degree or another, to the vapid pursuit of pleasure, sexual or otherwise. Now, it's beyond argument that both Christianity and Judaism preach the holy nature of chastity, and there is a reason. If pleasure becomes drug-like in its effect then it tends towards weakening the metaphysical aspects of the West's founding principles, thus undermining and delegitimizing them. This isn't an idle statement; it has been proven empirically to be a function of evolutionary psychology. In numerous studies, religious cults with many rules, strictly [not brutally] enforced, have a far better chance of surviving than those with a more laissez-faire approach.

One of the most powerful indictments that the jihadists level against us is that, "we love death more than you love life," meaning they claim to be more devout.

Though there are vast numbers of Muslims worldwide, many of them are so busy simply surviving, that they cling to their ideology with the type of fervor which the West hasn't seen since at least the 18th century, when Christianity was truly a living faith, the solid footing expressed in the idea of the, "rock of ages." Upon careful examination it goes even deeper than that; much of the Muslim world embraces a 10th century interpretation of Islam. If the West wanted to experience such strength of belief it would need to time travel back to Medieval Europe.

Consequently, it's not happenstance that the left pushes sensuality. When its importance in one's life rises to the point where the need for "sex, drugs and rock 'n roll," becomes all consuming we shouldn't be surprised to find an electorate so occupied with feeding its various desires that "simple things," such as maintaining critical thinking skills regarding the ideas which keep the West free, fall by the wayside.

This isn't necessarily to argue for asceticism, by any means. Humans have needs, wants and desires which really can't be suppressed beyond a certain level. When that boundary is crossed these forces find their way to the surface in ways which can easily be even more unhealthy, perhaps becoming sublimated/transferred into more destructive emotions such as violence. Within Islam we see this both internally and externally, for example in the belief's sacralized cruelty, internally against its own libertines and externally towards unbelievers, even if they are Muslim but of the wrong stripe.

So a reasonable but always imperfect balance must be struck - a cautionary note regarding the need to keep sensuality/licentiousness etc., under self-control. This is always a balancing act, but the results are always positive in that it yields a morally sober and responsible society, something which in large part the West no longer represents. As the traditions of the nation fade and lose meaning, so does its will to defend itself to survive.

The above exploration aside, in analyzing the nexus between these two menaces [which are quite literally a "united front"] the levels of affinity between Marxism and Islamism can be seen as a carapace of shared macro-values and goals:

Both are internationalist in the sense of seeing beyond borders; they seek the overthrow of the existing order and believe in perpetual struggle - note the symmetry between Marxist "wars of national liberation" and jihad. This very odd couple desires to impose, by force if necessary, utopian political/economic systems rooted in controlling the populace. These partners of convenience consider appeasement to be provocative and they share an unwavering and unshakeable sense of intellectual superiority/triumphalism - the belief that theirs is the inevitable pathway to what has been termed the "end of history."

The latter concept relies on the historicism of Hegel, which heavily influenced the young Marx. Finally, both systems advocate the redistribution of wealth, taking from the "rich nobles" [or the bourgeoisie] and giving it to the poor [exploited victims of capitalism].

> "At the time of the Prophet's call to Messengership, Arab society was devoid of proper distribution of wealth and devoid of justice. A small group monopolized all wealth and commerce, which increased through usury. The great majority of the people were poor and hungry. The wealthy were also regarded as noble and distinguished, and the common people were not only deprived of wealth but also of dignity and honor. It can be said that Muhammad - peace be upon him - was capable of starting a social movement, declaring war against the class of nobles and the wealthy, taking away their wealth and distributing it to the poor." [source, Seyyid Qutb, Milestones, p. 26-27].

Additionally, anti-Semitism/Jew hatred is a strong current in both of these ideologies. We feel no need to demonstrate this aspect of Islamism since it's on constant display, but with regard to Marxism a few examples should suffice because to Marx, the Jew was a "problem." He lives an insular life and refuses to recognize the authority of the state which in Hegelian analysis represents the fullest expression of man, of the "right" to use his term

In the various writings of Marx, which dealt with what he called the "Jewish Problem," the author's vicious anti-Semitism is anything but hidden:

"Money is the jealous god of Israel, in face of which no other god may exist. Money degrades all the gods of man - and turns them into commodities. Money is the universal self-established value of all things. It has, therefore, robbed the whole world - both the world of men and nature - of its specific value. Money is the estranged essence of man's work and man's existence, and this alien essence dominates him, and he worships it...the god of the Jews has become secularized and has become the god of the world. The bill of exchange is the real god of the Jew. His god is only an illusory bill of exchange...The view of nature attained under the domination of private property and money is a real contempt for, and practical debasement of, nature; in the Jewish religion, nature exists, it is true, but it exists only in imagination...What is the secular basis of Judaism? Practical need, self-interest. What is the worldly religion of the Jew? Huckstering. What is his worldly God? Money...Very well then! Emancipation from huckstering and money, consequently from practical, real Judaism, would be the self-emancipation of our time." [please refer to Pierre Birnbaum, The Geography of Hope, Exile, the Enlightenment, Disassimilation, Stanford University Press, 2008, pp 58-63]

Progressive leftism/Marxism and Islamism then are the chief ideologies which seek our destruction. They are the protagonists which drive transformational politics of the type we are now witness to in the West and in most of the Muslim world. They are complementary and operate in tandem fashion, allying where politically advantageous, knowing that they both wish to destabilize their quarry.

In the shadow war to overturn the culture, language is an essential component so naturally it becomes a target. Understandably then, conflict over the lexicon is being waged at the highest levels of the national security apparatus, throughout government as a whole and in a much more general and all encompassing sense, throughout the culture. The non-governmental institutions which have been targeted in this clandestine influence operation are those which define and create our way of life, culture and ultimately, our civilization.

Realizing that these represent the soft underbelly of a republican democracy they are under furious assault by the neo-Marxist left and their unholy revolutionary allies, the jihadists.

The concept is not a new one, *control the language, circumscribe the parameters within which dialogue is permissible...dominate the narrative, and therefore define the culture*. This technique has bled into academe, where it has found great resonance.

As an analogy think of the component narrative as being the particular, which in concert with others of the same nature, create the general which some might define as a meme.

In a real world example [Ferguson, Missouri] the fraudulent local narrative characterized by the slogan "hands up, don't shoot" is employed to set the stage for the larger cultural indictment that white law enforcement is engaged in a willful and systematic campaign of "hunting" young Black men. We will leave it to the good judgment of the reader to discern the foundational from the particular, keeping in mind that generally "fundamental transformation" hinges upon the degree of success in changing the metanarrative by manipulating its components.

We also ask the reader to comprehend that all of the HAMAS linked American Muslim organizations have identified with and signed on to the tenets of the Soros funded Black Lives Matter crowd.

The enemy of my enemy...

CHAPTER FIVE - ANTONIO GRAMSCI AND CULTURAL MARXISM

Antonio Gramsci was and largely remains an obscure 1930s era Italian Communist theoretician who was instrumental in developing the modern nomenclature of cultural transformation. His writings reveal extraordinary perceptual insight into how customs, language, religion/belief structures etc., might be changed, pushed as it were, in a direction that the culture would not normally have taken under its own inertia.

In the early part of the 20th century, Gramsci identified and explored the idea of changing the way a society perceived and thought about itself, its epistemology. He proposed a process - a slow and methodical "march" by the new standard bearers through the institutions - incrementally taking over and corrupting the foundations and mechanisms whereby culture is created and molded - the news and social media, the arts, the law, the edutocracy, government, organized religion...even science.

Nothing that contributes to the nature of a society would be left untouched. He reasoned that this would empower those who were engaged in the transfiguration to establish a new cultural "hegemony," to replace the "rotting corpse" of capitalists.

To say he was a voluminous writer would be denigrate his output; it was an activity in which he was always seemingly engaged. Reflective of this near obsession, Gramsci's theories became the cornerstone of economic Marxism's ugly twin, *cultural Marxism*, which is the most easily identifiable aspect of the ideology that's recognizable throughout the society today.

Successfully employed, the process cuts society from its moorings, binding citizens in Dostoevsky's contention - that if some ultimately authoritative source of truth doesn't exist, then everything is permitted, thus clearing the playing field for the social engineers and mischief makers.

"... It's God that's worrying me. That's the only thing that's worrying me. What if He doesn't exist? What if Rakitin's right - that it's an idea made up by men? Then if He doesn't exist, man is the chief of the earth, of the universe. Magnificent! Only how is he going to be good without God? That's the question. I always come back to that. For whom is man going to love then? To whom will he be thankful? To whom will he sing the hymn? [source, Part IV. Book XI: Ivan, Chapter 4: A Hymn and a Secret, The Brothers Karamazov, p. 1243]

In the case of Islam, adherents are very tightly regulated and severely punished for transgressions against the faith, but non-believers are essentially meat to be fed into the grinder. ISIS, Boko Haram and Al-Shabaab's "atrocities" are not anomalous; they are justified within the Qur'an and are therefore sacralized. The level of brutality with which these groups operate is incomprehensible to most Western minds. Since we have been engaged in covering these matters for so long now a certain amount of desensitization has necessarily taken place. As is the case with nearly all people working in this field, there are aspects relating to the global jihad that we refuse to publish because they are so hideous and unspeakably evil. Be advised however that those who are maximally committed to these ideologies will stop at absolutely nothing to bring their vision about and that unless one is very well-versed in these matters, it's impossible to imagine the level of depraved cruelty which these fanatics can summon to impose their will.

Lesson: the ideology will always trump any other consideration...period.

Both Marxism and Islamism reject the Western concept of revealed truth [in the Jeffersonian sense of wisdom bestowed by interacting with "nature's God" who does not dictate doctrine verbatim], of immutable moral precepts which originate at a level above man's existence, can be discovered through studied reason and imbue him with unalienable natural rights, including the freedom to choose one's religion, or reject it out of hand.

In the rarefied environment of a situational/cultural relativity, both Judaism and Christianity entirely lose their moral authority, the ability to provide guidance in human affairs. Why not then kill, or covet your neighbor's wife or goods? Why set aside a time of contemplation of things larger than yourself?

Under Gramsci's analysis, if the culture isn't "Marxist friendly," the solution is to engage in an engineering project [invoking the idea of the long or hundred year war] pushing the nucleus of the culture towards one which is less resistant to change. In Gramsci's way of looking at the mater one might begin with awakening the proletariat so that it would first, come to recognize its existence as an identifiable and oppressed class and then to create an awareness of its supposed role in society, its miserable plight, lowly status and then blame that state of affairs on capitalism. It was thought that the "workers," so indoctrinated would welcome the possibility of "being freed" and become foot soldiers in the revolution. The institutions chosen for radical transformation include the aforementioned entities, especially those at the top of the food chain which have a certain natural command authority.

In the introduction to the Cambridge Text in The History of Political Thought devoted to Gramsci's' pre-prison writings, editors Raymond Guess and Quentin Skinner outlined key aspects of his philosophy including the idea of "'hegemony' or ideological power, which forms the most distinctive feature of Marxism:

"[and] equally heretical was his emphasis on the role of ideas and the human will...The revolutionary wing of the Party [PSI, the Italian Socialist Party] typically adopted a more 'orthodox' Marxism that stressed the internal dynamics of the historical process and the necessary collapse of capitalism under its own contradictions...he stressed the need to educate and organize the collective will of the masses, preparing them for the coming revolution through the dissemination of new values that gave them a critical purchase on their current situation and galvanized them into action...even at this early stage, Gramsci had begun to formulate what was to become one of his most distinctive doctrines - the strategy of preparing for the revolutionary seizure of power by building a counter-state within the structure of civil society via a plethora of Party run organization." [Cambridge: Gramsci, p. xii-xiii]

Gramsci's ideas have a high degree of affinity with Lenin's theory of "dual power," defined as a growing revolutionary "proto state" operating outside of the extant governmental power structure. Organizationally, it's comprised of the ideologically grounded Marxist vanguard leadership and its shock troops [who are to a greater or lesser degree "politically enlightened" workers, i.e., the proletariat]. In outlook this nascent movement is proudly revolutionary, fully intending to come to power by forcibly seizing control:

"What is this dual power? Alongside the Provisional Government, the government of bourgeoisie, another government has arisen, so far weak and incipient, but undoubtedly a government that actually exists and is growing - the Soviets of Workers' and Soldiers' Deputies. What is the class composition of this other government? It consists of the proletariat and the peasants (in soldiers' uniforms). What is the political nature of this government? It is a revolutionary dictatorship, i.e., a power directly based on revolutionary seizure, on the direct initiative of the people from below, and not on a law enacted by a centralised state power. It is an entirely different kind of power from the one that generally exists in the parliamentary bourgeois-democratic republics of the usual type still prevailing in the advanced countries of Europe and America."

On hegemony, "The second usage refers more broadly to the organization of the cultural, moral and ideological consent of the population to the prevailing political and economic system through the institutions of civil society, such as schools, churches, parties etc." [p. xxxvii]

> "If every State tends to create and maintain a certain type of civilisation and of citizen (and hence of collective life and of individual relations), and to eliminate certain customs and attitudes and to disseminate others, then the Law will be its instrument for this purpose (together with the school system, and other institutions and activities). It must be developed so that it is suitable for such a purpose - so that it is maximally effective and productive of positive results." [p. 508]

In another example:

> "Political concept of the so-called "Permanent Revolution", which emerged before 1848 as a scientifically evolved expression of the Jacobin experience from 1789 to Thermidor [French for the summer months, 1793, the onset of the "Great Terror"]…In the period after 1870, with the colonial expansion of Europe, all these elements change: the internal and international organizational relations of the State become more complex and massive, and the Forty-Eightist [referring to the revolutions of 1848] formula of the "Permanent Revolution" is expanded and transcended in political science by the formula of "civil hegemony." [source, Selections from the Prison Notebooks, p. 502-503, ElecBook, London 1999, Essential Classics in Politics: Antonio Gramsci, EB 0006, ISBN 1 901843 05 X]

Of note, Trotsky was the chief proponent among the Marxist-Leninist intellectual class and leaders of the Bolsheviks who desired a permanent, never-ending revolution. In the odd logic which theoretical communists use, Trotsky admired the original spirit of the French Revolution's Jacobins, the concept of an ever-boiling political pot. When the bloodletting really started, he parted ways - for ideological, not humanitarian reasons, with the wild and escalating barbarism produced by Robespierre's

"Reign of Terror," which culminated in the execution of King Louis XVI and Queen Marie Antoinette.

To Trotsky, the process stultified the revolution. It wasn't that he was in any way against revolutionary violence, it's just that he felt that the direction it took - the revolution's blood feast which began in earnest in 1793 - brought an end to the unfolding political realignment.

Trotsky was blind to the contradiction that his politics ultimately required violence to succeed and that once set in motion it becomes an uncontrollable beast. Though speculative, one might surmise that he would have approved of Stalin's wide-scale murderous purges - which exceeded the "excesses" of the French Revolution by several orders of magnitude - since by that point in Soviet history, all opposition had been crushed and the revolution could proceed.

Many today find it remarkable and beyond understanding how the social bedrock [long established concepts, practices, institutions, etc.] have so easily been subverted by the enemies of the state. Actually it shouldn't be that mysterious; Gramsci and his fellow revolutionaries believed that everything is politics, the kernel that drives never-ending agitation. Facing off against a profoundly target-rich environment, there are always elemental cultural structures ripe for attack:

> "Is not science itself "political activity" and political thought, in as much as it transforms men, and makes them different from what they were before? If everything is "politics", then it is necessary...to distinguish by means of new concepts...the politics which corresponds to that science which is traditionally called "philosophy," and on the other the politics which is called political science in the strict sense." [p. 505]

This leads us to the current nature of science which, in modernity, has come to be a duality:

A. Legitimate science based upon the traditional means of ascertaining physical laws and truths: experimentation, the development of hypotheses and the formulations of theories which must be tested in the real world and if found wanting, rejected.

B. "Junk" science, funded by the government, NGOs or otherwise influenced, in which "facts" are massaged to arrive at a theory which has already been predetermined. The mark of phony science is that its theories are impossible to disprove and result in further empowerment of the state.

We see this reflected in the debate over man-made global warming [now rebranded under the all-encompassing term, "climate change" because of the impossibility of proving that anthropogenic global warming is taking place] for which the data has simply been either made-up or intentionally misinterpreted. The two aspects which most define this practice are one, that the money used towards the funding of such "research" is only provided on a quid-pro-quo basis; if the desired results are not produced, then the gravy train stops, and two, that state approved, but errant theories are then used as a political weapon to extend and/or enforce aspects of the revolution.

More astute observers of the new left will find the preceding confirmatory evidence of what they see every day; in a war for the culture there is nothing - not even the most well established principles, concepts or beliefs [traditional marriage for example] that cannot be given a political spin which makes it fair game to be contested and therefore redefined.

Often, especially in political philosophy, there can be a chasm between practice and theory, however in the case of Gramsci the techniques which he developed and clarified, the correspondence is quite close, the very reason he is such an important figure in this discussion.

This is why the Soviet Communists devoted so much energy in attacking and undermining American culture knowing it is the West's standard bearer of republicanism.

It should be understood that Gramsci operated in a sealed bubble world of intellectualism. Think of it as the difference between theorist and the net product of the process itself, of scientist and engineer. The former spends a lifetime in the fascinating pursuit of ideas and concepts, the latter objectifies them in order that they may be put into practice in the real world.

The Union of Soviet Socialist Republics, the USSR, was a case in point, it having been the actualization of philosophies which might have sound intriguing to many, promising as they did, a new world where strife, inequality and injustice no longer existed.

Those, however who have taken any time to survey the historical period from the October Revolution to the dissolution of the Soviet state in 1991 can see how dissimilar the promises of Marxist-Leninist political philosophy/ideology are from their concrete application.

The messianic aspect of communism drove those charged with spreading the doctrine on a world-wide basis to enlist thousands of bright Russians, mostly young students into the equivalent of the Soviet priesthood, the KGB. This service operated domestically as the secret police [the KGB was a branch of the military] and outside mother Russia as an intentionally prosaic looking espionage agency. However to the surprise of many the most important duty these people had was to function as practitioners of disinformation and psychological warfare [agitprop], intent upon subverting "enemy" cultures.

Once in the West it became even clearer to KGB agents with any acuity at all, that the Soviet dream was a lie. As a result defection became, if not common, unsurprising. Sometimes, fearing for the fate of friends and family which remained inside the prison state, agents would just "disappear," leaving no trace which would brand them as turn-coats and thus subject their loved ones to the wrath of Soviet authorities.

One of those defectors was Yuri Bezmenov who before escaping the system worked as a press operative, engaged in presenting an idealized version of communism to a lapdog media.

But once secure in his new surroundings, Bezmenov took it upon himself to explain the process of cultural subversion which clearly demonstrates the practical application of Gramsci's theories. This spy who "came in from the cold," stressed that undermining a society depended first and most importantly on the ability to demoralize an enemy.

"Demoralization takes [a minimum of] 15-20 years to educate a generation of students in the country of your enemy exposed to the ideology of the enemy. Marxist-Leninist ideology is being pumped into the soft heads of at least three generations of American students without being challenged or counter-balanced by the basic values of Americanism, American patriotism

The result? The result you can see; most of the people who graduated in the 60s, drop-outs or half-baked intellectuals are now occupying the positions of power in the government, civil service, business, mass media and the educational system

You are stuck with them, you can't get rid of them, they are contaminated, they are programmed to think and react to certain stimuli in certain patterns. You cannot change their minds even if you expose them to authentic information even if you prove to them that white is white and black is black you still cannot change the basic perception and the logical behavior. The process of demoralization is complete and irreversible. To get society free of these people you need another 20 or 15 years to educate a new generation of patriotically minded and common sense people who would be acting in favor and in the interest of the United States society." [source, transcript of video, KGB Psychological Warfare and Cultural Subversion of the West, testimony from ex-PGU/KGB agent Yuri Alexandrovich Bezmenov.]

The theories of multiculturalism and diversity [center-pieces of cultural Marxism] and their practice, arguably are the most powerful drivers of modern transformational politics because they blunt the effectiveness of the process whereby a society can maintain its unique nature. They are roadblocks designed to thwart assimilation, acculturation and integration, the schemata which has created the essence of what it means to be a [non-hyphenated] American.

Within the Gramscian dialectic, multiculturalism, diversity and "cultural pluralism" become spiritualized stratagems of class [and its sub-genres, gender, ethnic, sexual identification, etc.] warfare. Imagine the many layers of an onion, interspersed with shards of glass, each working against the other to reduce the object into a formless mass. They inevitably [and are designed to] lead to Balkanized cultures. This battle has largely been uncontested over the last 100 years, the primary reason for its strong presence in academia since at least the late 1960s. [see, http://www.edchange.org/multicultural/papers/edchange_history. html]

None of this has a positive impact on the security of the nation…or the culture.

Over the years this class/ethnic consciousness of "separateness" has been forced into the primary and secondary schools as well as worming its way into other secular and even religious institutions. Multiculturalists rejoice in creating an atomized polity, a melting pot in reverse. That realization is significant, since it identifies multiculturalism as part of a larger political movement which is internationalist in nature and revolutionary in scope because it can be used to simultaneously attack all of Western Civilization.

The multi-cultists aren't shy about stating their ambitiously radical goal of wholesale change. We quote at considerable length from the National Association of Multicultural Education.

Yes, there is indeed such a body and we include so much of the text because it embraces ideas which not that long ago would have been rejected out of hand as being crazy:

"Multicultural education is a philosophical concept built on the ideals of freedom, justice, equality, equity, and human dignity as acknowledged in various documents, such as the U.S. Declaration of Independence, constitutions of South Africa...it affirms our need to prepare students for their responsibilities in an interdependent world. It recognizes the role schools can play in developing the attitudes and values necessary for a democratic society. It values cultural differences and affirms the pluralism that students, their communities, and teachers reflect. It challenges all forms of discrimination in schools and society through the promotion of democratic principles of social justice...it prepares all students to work actively toward structural equality in organizations and institutions by providing the knowledge, dispositions, and skills for the redistribution of power and income among diverse groups. Thus, school curriculum must directly address issues of racism, sexism, classism, linguicism, ablism, ageism, heterosexism, religious intolerance, and xenophobia...teachers and students must critically analyze oppression and power relations in their communities, society and the world...Multicultural education requires comprehensive school reform as multicultural education must pervade all aspects of the school community and organization. Recognizing that equality and equity are not the same thing, multicultural education attempts to offer all students an equitable educational opportunity, while at the same time, encouraging students to critique society in the interest of social justice." [source, NAME]

This is the core of multicultural thinking - a code-word laden defense of an intentionally divisive identity politics. In this case inspired, by of all things, the South African Constitution and similar UN declarations and charters all of which shed further light on its true nature. It's a philosophy which is totally at odds with the shared beliefs, traditions and body of laws which have guided America since its founding.

A few selected passages from the South African, post Apartheid, constitution:

It writes inequality and unequal treatment into the law - *"To promote the achievement of equality, legislative and other measures designed to protect or advance persons, or categories of persons, disadvantaged by unfair discrimination may be taken."*

The document disregards freedom of expression - *" [it] does not extend to propaganda for war, incitement of imminent violence or advocacy of hatred that is based on race, ethnicity, gender or religion."*

It doesn't recognize private property - *"Property may be expropriated only in terms of law of general application... [it may be expropriated]...for a public purpose or in the public interest... the public interest includes the nation's commitment to land reform, and to reforms to bring about equitable access to all South Africa's natural resources; and property is not limited to land ... The state must take reasonable legislative and other measures, within its available resources, to foster conditions which enable citizens to gain access to land on an equitable basis."*

This is a legal corpus which absolutely guarantees violence. It's the charter of a police state, which is evident even upon a brief review of how the South African government behaves on a daily basis.

"In July of 2012, Dr. Gregory Stanton, head of the nonprofit group Genocide Watch, conducted a fact-finding mission in South Africa. He concluded that there is a coordinated campaign of genocide being conducted against white farmers, known as Boers. "The farm murders, we have become convinced, are not accidental," Stanton contended. "It was very clear that the massacres were not common crimes," he added -- especially because of the absolute barbarity used against the victims...It is a post-liberation effort that remains alarmingly on track to emulate all the other historically blood-soaked efforts by Marxists, who invariably need an enemy at whom to direct their anger. White African farmers are that enemy." [source, Arnold Ahlert, The Gruesome Reality of Racist South Africa, FrontPage Magazine, warning extremely graphic content]

The tenets of multiculturalism are really stalking horses, masquerading as the agents of "social," "political," "economic," and "educational" justice, all of which operate in a manner opposite to the lofty imagery they are crafted to connote.

Equity in the above sense [equality of outcome, or shared misery] is really the process the Founders excoriated as "leveling." It bluntly empowers Leviathan government and given enough time and resources the megalith becomes impossibly strong - impregnable - leaving only two options: violence or subjugation.

Enslavement is clearly unacceptable but revolutionary violence is only slightly less so.

If as a "Yankee" you have ever spent much time with the "Rebs" in the Heart of Dixie it's impossible not to see how the scars from the Civil War [the "War of Northern Aggression"] have failed to fully heal, despite the passage of 150 years, 8 generations. The societal dislocation that would result from an all encompassing revolt are unimaginable and the outcome would be completely uncontrollable. Once the shooting started things would never, ever be the same. If we were somehow to survive such a cataclysm, 500 years from now it would remain as the most significant event in American history.

The left, supremacist pseudo-religions, the educational gulag [from which this theory has been spread like a plague] and racial separatists who hasten its acceptance - have found safe harbor within the Democrat Party. As we are currently witnessing, these people are willing to break whole truck loads of eggs in order to sustain Trotsky's perpetual revolution, despite the fact that many, perhaps most, have no idea of the process' intellectual origin.

Perhaps the members of the Students for a Democratic Society [a Marxist coven comprised of hippie-era spoiled upper class college misfits] encapsulated the process most concisely, *"the issue is NEVER the issue, the issue is ALWAYS the revolution."* For readers so inclined we refer you to the SDS' Port Huron Manifesto, issued in 1962 and written by Tom Hayden, who probably needs no introduction, except possibly to note that he was one of the prominent leaders [married for a while to fellow revolutionary Jane Fonda] who helped the final push in which the Marxists took over the Democrat Party.

Though it may be obvious to some it's worth knowing that the SDS leftists "revolution" is just another shorthand example of Trotsky's more theoretically precise terminology.

It's this never-ending, churning process of social upheaval to which the modern progressive/neo-Marxists are heir. Always be mindful that truly revolutionary ideologies [this includes Islamism] bridle at the thought of concession or half-measures. Their demands always exceed society's capacity to accommodate and this is by design. It's typified in the popular revolutionary slogan, "we want the world and we want it now." Though they won't abide anything but total victory, these people are above all patient and blindingly full of themselves in the belief that the way of life they wish to impose on everyone else is an historical inevitability. This accounts for the endless negotiations in which they participate, while clandestinely continuing to chip at foundational elements.

We call the reader's attention to a recent case study [source, WTF File Vol. I No. II - Ex-Chair of Brit 'Human Rights Commission" Shocked: Muslims Won't Assimilate, April 11, 2016, PipeLineNews.org] which relates the story of how a once high-flying British bureaucrat, manipulated British culture to literally create the term Islamophobia. He did this with clear purpose, intending to then monetarily farm, through various organizations, consultancies and agencies, this freshly plowed field. The techniques used by Mr. Phillips as described below seem to have been lifted directly from Gramsci's playbook:

"Though the party in question, Trevor Phillips, is now attempting to publicly distance himself from the multicultural Islamist horse-shit he force fed the British public during his stormy tenure as the excessively compensated chair of the country's Equality and Human Rights Commission, upon investigation, his spiel rings false. After looking at his long shady record, actually Phillips seems to mostly be concerned with rebranding himself as a born again anti-Islamist.

'Phillips commissioned "the Runnymede report" into Britain and Islamophobia in 1997 which, according to both Phillips himself and academics across the country, popularised the phrase which has now become synonymous with any criticism - legitimate or not - of Islam or Muslims.' [source, Raheem Kassam, UK Equalities Chief Who Popularised The Term 'Islamophobia' Admits: 'I Thought Muslims Would Blend into Britain , Breitbart]

But in order to better grasp the flow of events here, let's step back nearly 20 years, where we learn that it was Phillips who - far more than merely commissioning a study, which we are led to believe got a bit sideways - ran the lefty think tank which got the ball rolling. The Runnymede report was generated by an organization, the Runnymede Trust, which in turn created the

Commission on British Muslims and Islamophobia, which then issued the report.

This is the typical leftist shell-game, concealing linkages as to give the look of propriety to propaganda. According to the organization's Wiki, Phillips chaired Runnymede from 1993-1998, the operative time-frame during which the "report" and "Islamophobia" were injected into the intellectual marketplace Of note, even the notoriously progressive Wiki characterized Runnymede as "a left-wing think tank."

So it might be said that Phillips created the market in which the EHRC [at least temporarily] thrived, as from the outset the organization generated controversy. As Chair of EHRC he was paid £160,000 on a pro-rata basis [considerably more than the British PM] with compensation adjusted according to a planned for eventually less than full-time role by the Chair.

If one were asked to describe the outfit it would be charitable to say that EHRC was so chronically mismanaged during Phillips' watch - 2006-2012 - that, fairly quickly it lost all credibility as well as half of its funding and staff, a development almost unheard of in modern bureaucracies.

> "The Equality and Human Rights Commission has been stripped of its duty to promote a society with equal opportunity for all and had its budget and workforce halved, the government has announced. The move comes days after the watchdog chided ministers for failing to consider how crucial policies would affect women, disabled people and ethnic minorities. The EHRC has long been a bugbear for the Tory right who see it as a relic of the past. It has also been criticised by MPs for financial mismanagement after the National Audit Office (NAO) refused to sign off the commission's accounts for three years in a row." [source, Equality and Human Rights Commission has workforce halved , UK Guardian]

More to the point are the strong hints of corruption/conflicts of interest attending Phillips' stewardship which were considered so grave that a formal investigation by Parliament was instituted.

Chief among the concerns was Phillips having set up a private consultancy group - Equate Organisation - which provided counsel for profit to the same universe of organizations which fell subject to the social justice warriors at EHRC.

"Mr. Phillips is also the co-founder of the Equate Organisation, which was incorporated in February 2007. This is a consultancy specialising in the management of diversity. Its website, http://www.equate.org.uk, prominently features a picture of Mr. Phillips on every page and identifies him as chair of the EHRC, as well as "one of the leading experts on equality and diversity policy in Europe". Such expertise must be important for Equate, since Mr. Phillips' co-founder, Charles Armitage, is described as "a respected media entrepreneur specialising in maximising intellectual property and talent management", and would seem to have no particular qualifications to advise on equality and diversity." [source, Michael Rubenstein, Trevor Phillips Moonlights, Michael Rubenstein Publishing]

The official investigation however is a bit more damning. Throughout the affair Phillips was evasive and it was not until pressed hard by those conducting the inquiry that he reluctantly provided the initially asked for information, albeit after having been backed into a corner.

The following testimony relates to the obvious conflict of interest involved in Phillips chairing a government organization while being involved in an outside group which promised to remediate the type of charges which EHRC could level:

"Q137 Lord Lester of Herne Hill: Could I ask about conflicts of interest? You are the co-founder of the Equate Organisation consultancy.

Mr. Phillips: Correct.

Q138 Lord Lester of Herne Hill: I think you are a majority shareholder?

Mr. Phillips: I am not now. I was as at the beginning but I am not now.

Q139 Lord Lester of Herne Hill: Dr Brewer, the chief executive, it seems from what we have read, repeatedly tried to persuade you to stand down from the Equate consultancy to remove the perceived conflict of interest between your function as Chair of the Commission and your private financial interest. Is that correct?

Mr. Phillips: No…

Q141 Lord Lester of Herne Hill: You did not hear my question, I think. My question was whether it was right that the chief executive repeatedly sought to persuade you to remove the perceived conflict of interest and you said that is not right, but are you sure about that?

Mr. Phillips: The chief executive gave me advice about this, as did the Commission's own lawyers and, indeed, my own lawyers.

Q142 Lord Lester of Herne Hill: What was their advice?

Mr. Phillips: That there would be a perceived conflict of interest. [source from Equality and Human Rights Commission, Thirteenth Report of Session 2009-10, p. 67-8]

Nothing about Phillips rings true since it was his intention to create an industry which he then set out to thoroughly exploit; so rather than be celebrated as a singular voice of [repentant] reason from the British Isles, he should be seen for what he is, a self-promoting charlatan, incapable of telling the truth. We expect to see Phillips on the rubber chicken lecture circuit soon along with other frauds such as fellow Brit, Maajid Nawaz, a professional taqiyya artist."

So as should be apparent, modifying with an eye towards radically changing cultural narratives isn't that difficult, assuming one has sufficient official stature and power to pull the levers along with the political skill to execute such a devious plan.

That said we would like to shift the focus a bit, to an issue that might at first glance appear to be of questionable merit in this discussion, U.S. currency, specifically, paper money.

Since the mid 19th century, U.S. greenbacks have prominently displayed the images of important political figures, especially presidents, all of whom just happen to be men, really not that controversial since it's based upon the recognition that the country was founded and built by men – white males of European extraction, at that.

Though over time some of the images have changed, the circulation of billions in legal tender with the likenesses of famous individuals constitute an important element in the iconography of America, representing and combining elements of four of Jung's archetypes: the hero, the ruler, the wise man and the creator.

Because handling cash is so commonplace - though it's quickly being supplanted by electronic transfer of funds - it looms as a powerful form of subliminal advertising. It reinforces the overall cultural narrative as to what is valued, and given the omnipresence of exchange, gains import as the elemental monetized commodity, one only issuable by the U.S. Treasury Department.

As such these pictograms bolster tradition with every transaction.

But the forces of societal engineering never sleep, forever concocting new methods of destroying history and creating new associations, in this instance with a trio of our ancient "patriarchs" slated for symbolic execution at the hands of the left's created female heroes.

With Harriet Tubman eventually slated to replace President Andrew Jackson on the $20 dollar bill, she will eventually be joined by a gaggle of other female social-justice types such as Sojourner Truth, Susan B. Anthony, Elizabeth Cady Stanton, Alice Paul, Lucretia Mott and opera singer Marian Anderson. [source Samantha Masunaga, Harriet Tubman is the next face of the $20 bill; $5 and $10 bills will also change, LA Times]

But what list of this nature would be complete without Eleanor Roosevelt, who is famous not simply because her husband was FDR but because it seems to be an open secret that she was a lesbian...of course begging the question of when Hillary will get her turn...

While people pay almost no conscious attention to the pictoral content of their folding money all of that would change amidst the whipped-up drama of introducing the public to a new currency featuring the images of people, most of whom are deservedly a footnote in history.

Much like reality television, these people are famous because...well they are famous and therefore become fixtures in the social consciousness.

Never mind that the CV's of some of the counter-culture's rising stars are more than a bit thin and that the leadoff batter in the always contact sport of political warfare, Harriet Tubman, who though undoubtedly was Black, was also an accomplice of the axe murdering domestic terrorist/abolitionist, John Brown whose crazed "insurrection" resulted in the killing of nearly two dozen, including at least two Blacks.

Not wanting to upset sensitive readers unnecessarily, whose only understanding of Brown's demented mini-revolution is the lyric inspired by the bloody uprising, "John Brown's Body Lies a Moldering in the Grave" [set to the tune of the Battle Hymn of the Republic, giving it a certain patriotic - however misplaced - flavor], several of Brown's first victims - who did not own slaves - were gruesomely tortured to death with knives and axes.

Yet the left and other forces which are slowly destroying the West will use the debut of the new money to insinuate the newly created, state approved iconography, as sacred totems into the unsuspecting culture at large.

In advertising the process is known as registration, in this case through incessant product placement, creating a positive feeling or reaction to an object and/or idea as part of the branding process.

By this point we trust that the reader clearly understands the highly ductile nature of society…how events become symbols, then assume mythic proportions - despite their lack of historical veracity - and are then used as tools by the social transformers to more fully render their utopian edifice.

The foregoing being the key to understanding the transformative process, another illustration might be instructive, though for some it may prove somewhat shocking - given the subject, who is totally undeserving of the sainthood since ingloriously bestowed upon him.

Though the truth is devastating to the most iconic American civil rights leader, Dr. Martin Luther King's journey from idealistic Christian pacifism to Marxist/Maoist revolutionary is probably best seen as a process, not excused by but certainly reinforced by the environment and times in which he worked. We use the word process implying a gradual evolution of his core beliefs over time. Though it may well be the case that his radical bent was part of his intellectual structure from a very early time, we cannot say for sure one way or another and for our purposes the answer to that question is really immaterial, in that it really doesn't speak to the issue at hand.

Facts are, as they say stubborn things and the truth is that King, though a professed Christian was a notorious serial womanizer and plagiarizer in his writings making his sanctimonious representations of faith hollow recitations which he did not nearly come close to practicing.

J. Edgar Hoover's hard-edged FBI was of course aware of King's "carrying-ons," but was far more concerned about his intimate ties to supporters of the Soviet Union, including, specifically Stanley Levison who was a central leader in the Communist Party USA at a time when the Stalinist organization was under the direct control of the Soviets.

Given Levison's affiliation with the radical left, to which he freely admitted in public Congressional testimony, it's impossible to imagine that King was unaware of his ideology. Levison wasn't a part time on-and-off source of counsel. He was in fact King's closest advisor. He personally took charge of King's flailing organization - the Southern Christian Leadership Conference [SCLC] - and turned it into a powerhouse. For a time he also served as King's literary agent and ghosted many of King's writings.

We think that it's undeniable that from a fairly early time in his political career, Dr. King was a Marxist, but craftily slowly rolled out his public support for the communist's "wars of national liberation," such as Vietnam. As a reference on this point please consider King's, Beyond Vietnam: A Time to Break Silence, April 4, 1967.

Reflecting a real ideological progression or totally engineered so as not to shock his followers, King's public statement radically changed over the space of about 10 years, from 1956 when he pleaded for non-violence with an angry crowd after his home had been bombed [he had previously received late night telephone calls conveying death threats] to King's role serving as Ho Chi

Minh's de-facto American "minister without portfolio."

Remarking upon King's true identity:

> "Moreover, King was a radical leftist. He promoted socialism, pacifism and the appeasement of totalitarian communism. He opposed the Vietnam War and even openly supported the Viet Cong and North Vietnam's Marxist dictator Ho Chi Minh, praising them as anti-imperialists battling Western occupying powers." [source, Jeffrey T. Kuhner, Martin Luther King's Mixed Legacy, Washington Times, September 1, 2011]

Nearly mirroring King's rise, another Black man, Malcolm Little, was also transforming his life. While serving a prison sentence for theft he grew more reflective, in short order joining the American Muslim group, the Nation of Islam. After his release from prison, and blessed with natural political and communication skills, he assumed a leadership position as the group's spokesman until the middle sixties, when disenchantment and radicalism overtook him.

Little then converted to Sunni Islam, taking on the name el-Hajj Malik el-Shabazz and later adopting the politicized name, Malcolm X. In observance of his new faith he spent time in the Arabic world and completed the hajj, the ritual Islamic duty [one of the 5 Pillars of Islam] to visit Mecca at least once in a lifetime.

Malcolm X formed his own mosque and assembly stressing "self-defense," in the face of what was largely Democrat led racist violence in the Deep South - be mindful that the KKK was the Democrat Party's military wing. Malcolm X refused to reject nonviolence, one of his favorite lines being, "by any means necessary" - a term which has gained urgency today, having been adopted by the new Black separatist/revolutionary movement, Black Lives Matters.

Malcolm X's primary role in the political dynamic of Black America is that he formally rejected King's professed non-violent narrative [we say professed because of his embrace of Marxist political warfare overseas] into the legitimizing of Black political violence.

Other militant Black leaders arose in this same time period, the self-admitted violent revolutionary group, the Black Panthers was founded in Oakland, CA in 1966. The Panthers were killers plain and simple, street thugs who wrapped their violence in a self-righteous political ideology who advocated "offing the pigs."

We believe that it was in this atmosphere that King no longer saw the need to hide his radical ideology. Classifying King's beliefs within the communist framework cannot be done with great precision. We have seen no evidence that he understood or intensely studied Marxism from a theoretical standpoint, so he might be considered a non-denominational mixture of Marx/Lenin, Mao and Trotsky.

As one can intuit from King's historical metamorphous - if he was not from a much earlier period already a communist - the historical period in which he operated was designer made to support such "changes of heart."

This is the essence, the outline of the Gramscian model, a strategic plan to engineer a society in which Marxism becomes the natural "progressive" final solution. For some it might also be helpful to see the matter as a process of ideological colonization. In Islamic ideology this dynamic is termed "jihad by hijrah," Arabic for conquest by occupation.

CHAPTER SIX - THE FAIRY TALE OF RIGOBERTA MENCHU

What follows, we hope will tie some of these possibly disparate sounding ideas together; we therefore submit the tale of Rigoberta Menchu.

Over the last 30 plus years the story of this Guatemalan Indian native woman has been a cause célèbre among the multiculturalists and intellectual class.

Menchu offered a fable - a sweeping morality play - in which a poor but brave native Latin American voice bore witness to the damaging nature of American imperialism in her country. In recognition of her story, she was awarded the Pulitzer Peace Prize in 1992. She was feted and lionized as a culture warrior for striking a blow against Uncle Sam's supposed predation on Guatemala's indigenous people.

Unfortunately for Menchu and her supporters, *I Rigoberta Menchu, An Indian Woman In Guatemala [1983],* has been conclusively proven to be a collection of untruths.

Her fabrications were demolished by anthropologist David Stoll - among others - who spent a great deal of time in the exact locations and villages that Menchu referred to and could find little if any corroboration between her statements and reality. Dr. Stoll's research was so overwhelming that the New York Times - seldom thought of as an agent of the vast right wing conspiracy - felt comfortable airing Stoll's side of the "controversy," despite it cutting across the grain of the Times' default, anti-Western narrative:

> "Says Stoll, "We have an unfortunate tendency to idolize native voices that serve our own political and moral needs, as opposed to others that do not." By constructing what Stoll calls "mythologies of purity," academics were able to

isolate themselves from the reality of a situation often at the expense of the people they were mythologizing. And this is exactly what he thought was happening in Guatemala and why, despite the risks, Stoll felt the moral imperative to "deconstruct" Rigoberta's story. It wasn't all that hard to do. Other than her age, twenty-three at the time of the narrative, just about every other contention in the book is conspicuously false." [source, Jack Cashil, Rigoberta Menchu Won The Nobel Too, American Thinker]

What was Menchu's motive?

She concocted the story to foster support for the Communist insurrection in Guatemala, and her subsequent tours of Europe in support of revolutionary politics testified to her purpose.

Mere fraud, however, wasn't enough to dissuade the PBS program *"Point of View"* from preparing multicultural lesson plans prominently featuring Ms. Menchu's forged reality, and to this day her book remains a leftist icon. This is typical of media's efforts to support "the movement" at all costs, especially as it relates to venerating it's version of patron saints.

> "[Multicultural education] fosters an animus against what are perceived as Western values, particularly the value placed on acquiring knowledge, on analytical thinking, and on academic achievement itself." - Losing Our Language How Multicultural Classroom Instruction Is Undermining Our Children's Ability to Read, Write, and Reason - Sandra Stotsky, Harvard Graduate School of Education. Also please refer to, Anne C. Westwater, William J. Bennetta , Review of "Losing Our Language", The Textbook League]

Unsurprisingly, formerly mandated Western civilization courses in higher education have in large part been strangled out of existence by practitioners of transformational politics, because though they assert the ancient wisdom associated with America's founding patriarchs, the authors are no longer around to defend their beliefs. Towards that end, Menchu's concocted anti-American paean against capitalism helped ignite the overturning of the long established model of a traditional education, steeped in imparting a body of common knowledge including the classical works of antiquity to produce a well-rounded citizen with an understanding and appreciation for a unique way of life.

As such it's a pivotal work.

That, *I Rigoberta Menchu*, is based on an act of intentional misrepresentation, and that its purveyors are aware of that fact, remarkably, does nothing to reduce its value as a leftist totem.

> "I think Rigoberta Menchu has been used by the right to negate the very important space that multiculturalism is providing in academia," says Marjorie Agosin, head of the Spanish department at Wellesley College. "Whether her book is true or not, I don't care. We should teach our students about the brutality of the Guatemalan military and the U.S. financing of it." [source, Wilson, Robin. "A Challenge to The Veracity of a Multicultural Icon," The Chronicle of Higher Education, 15 January 1999, pp. A14-A16].

We note with great emphasis the use of the term "icon" which attests to the secular religiosity with which the culture warriors hold this doctrine.

This mindset is eerily reminiscent of ex-CBS star reporter Dan Rather as he continued to insist that his forged document story on George Bush's National Guard duty remained relevant despite the fact that it was entirely made-up. The "Rather Standard" being: demonstrably fraudulent but nonetheless true.

Encapsulated, Rigoberta Menchu's fable is a blood libel against Western democracies. Her assertions were created out of whole cloth, a conclusion supported by Stoll's painstaking, scientifically valid, peer reviewed anthropological research.

Even significant elements in the leftist media trashed her thesis. Her brother wasn't burned alive by the Guatemalan army and none of the pivotal events she relates happened. The truth is that Menchu is simply another in a long line of Marxist propagandists intent upon advancing a twisted political cause. Not only are most of the book's events made up, the story itself is poorly told and less than expertly edited. It gains whatever power it has because its gullible, self-hating largely Caucasian audience is so foolish to simply accept, as a matter of faith, the ridiculous assertion that "native voices" have special access to wisdom, that it is easily deluded.

Multicultural education is learning devoid of worth; supposed uniqueness elevated over value. It goes far beyond the simple admonition to be respectful of those who come from differing cultures and ends up as a political tactic calculated to set groups at each other's throats, all to gain political advantage.

Actually it's an exceedingly clever tactic, similar in manner to the way in which diminutive hyenas successfully pursue large African plains game such as Wildebeest and huge 1,000 lb Eland. Individually, such relatively small creatures are powerless to bring down massive, tough and swift animals on their own, but assaults in packs - the animal kingdom's equivalent of gang warfare - as mirrored by the left's own rainbow coalition hunting parties - multiplies the effect of individual ferocity into a lethal weapon capable of bringing down far bigger game.

Lesson: hunting in packs becomes a "force multiplier" in military jargon, the effect is greater than the sum of constituent parts.

Multiculturalism should be understood as nothing less than a search and destroy mission directed against the majority culture all the while disguised to appeal to the basic fairness and tolerance which resides in the American spirit.

Where is the evidence that a strong multicultural education is superior? Everywhere it has been tried it has only succeeded in

98

less knowledgeable students and a lowering of academic achievement. Are there examples of nations based upon disunity, unclear purpose and Tower of Babel confusion having been successful?

The lessons of history preach distinctly the opposite.

Further complicating the picture, the educative process whereby multicultural diversity is imposed on impressionable young minds has become big business; the foundations, educational pressure groups, college departments and media busy bodies that support it are bathed in the mother's milk of activism, money, much of it flowing from an ever expanding centralized government.

Nearly every school district in the United States has a determined, well financed group of Zulu shock troops pushing this failed, inherently bigoted theory.

CHAPTER SEVEN - THE ART OF LINGUISTIC AND CONCEPTUAL WARFARE

Having already reviewed the general outline and some of the workings of the Gramscian model of establishing a culture more receptive to leftist political hegemony in chapter five, it's our purpose hereafter to demonstrate and illustrate how those theories have wide applicability. Naturally these techniques and methods are directed towards influencing the public or collective consciousness, inventing new relationships, patterns of linkage, motifs, symbols, icons, etc., which are then absorbed, almost by osmosis to produce a reconstructed societal gestalt.

Some might term it rewiring the American psyche, others, more direct, will call it devouring the culture.

This activity takes place at a more elemental level than rote propagandizing, generally the purview of the classroom via the pedagogical model. In that setting it's used to affirm or fix the new hegemonic ideals rather than create them - the job of the intellectual class, the central nervous system of the edutocracy.

The success of the effort doesn't demand that those so engaged are even aware of what is essentially informed speculation about how language and perception inter-relate with each other. All that is necessary is that through observation the techniques are understood as a matter of cause and effect.

In the same sense, one who goes out for a meal doesn't need to understand the chemistry of salt to appreciate its use as a seasoning.

Though beyond the scope of this book, some of these concepts are part of a larger, more technical discipline defined by philosopher Jerry A. Fodor as the "language of thought," [see Jerry Fodor, The Language of Thought Revisited, p. 21] and fall within the purview of semiotics, an area of linguistics which looks at how symbols [as mental constructs] affect perception. These hypotheses are undoubtedly subject to interpretation but there is merit in considering the nature of the idealized whole because of its probative value.

Those involved in refashioning of the West's internal organizing principles - its constituent components - are using an analytical method called structuralism, a tool, the purpose of which is to disassemble language into its sub-atomic component pieces so that they can be individually isolated, micro-manipulated and then...weaponized.

In exactly the same manner that an explosive device requires a method of ignition, a detonator - the Marxist/progressives as well as their allies, the Muslim Brotherhood civilizational jihadists, sensed that the near panic which followed the September 11, 2001 attacks presented them with a unique opportunity to push a highly unsettled America towards the grand vision of radical transformation they sought. Of course to be clear, the details of their respective endgames are wildly disparate aside from the central shared desire to obliterate American traditionalism.

The realization was almost immediately apparent, growing out of observing how the social dynamic responded to new stimuli and the general tendency of extremist organizations to always be probing for vulnerabilities.

Realignment is inherently the goal in the politics of deconstruction, taking advantage of an overwrought populace by appealing to its base emotions such as greed and envy, thus setting people against each other to weaken, destabilize and reprogram the central organizing [traditional] core.

What had come to be defined as the Marxist-Leninist principle of class warfare previously consisted of groups that were already widely recognized - those based upon wealth, ethnicity, geographical location, age, religion, etc., but post 911, the process became open-ended.

It's hard to overestimate the value of expanding the zone of conflict to encompass archetypes independent of historical frames of reference. Observing that interrelationships could transcend existing models - alchemies that didn't yet exist - it then became clear that they could be intentionally created.

In a manner of speaking the societal flux inherent in a mass casualty attack promised virtual access to the American psyche, from where it could be reprogrammed, a more technical implementation of Gramsci's ideas regarding how to quicken the rise of the nascent, ruling class.

The mindset of those who are participating in this continuous aggression assumes great importance as the Islamist/Marxist alliance advances. This is not a casual, part-time endeavor for them. *Revolution is their "day-job"* - non kinetic to be sure, at least while they are still in the minority - but a series of strategic initiatives nonetheless.

This enemy always comes to the fight dedicated to attaining total victory, an attitude of relentless belligerence. Using game theory to optimally maximize an effective offense, they set about to quickly establish the terms of the engagement, forcing the "enemy" to operate reactively. Here they have the same natural advantage that all insurgents possess; a concrete entity to attack. Much like the siege of a medieval castle, an attrition based conflict once established makes counter-attack impossible without leaving the relative safety provided by yards-thick stone walls.

There is another similarity between transformational conflict and previous modes of warfare. The Marxist/Islamist confederation is using historically proven techniques - campaigns designed to wear or grind an enemy down work, which provide them with the luxury of being able to choose the time and place where blood can then methodically be drawn.

No prisoners are taken and no quarter given. Mirroring the type of conflict that plagued Europe for nearly a millennia, they operate on a simple genocidal principle, "kill them all and let someone else sort them out."

This draws into acute focus a serious issue: when one ponders why the opposition, which still commands a numerical majority, at least in the United States - aside from the craven self interest displayed by the GOP and its parrot-like beltway prognosticators - doesn't strike back, the structural problem of being the target looms as a constant impediment.

Looking back over the last 15 years - an eternity considering the changing face of a metamorphosed nation - we must recall what the immediate reaction was to the events of that clear, slightly chilly but sunny Tuesday morning in September.

Shock, disbelief at first, then the overwhelming sense of horror and rage as the Towers continued to burn, buckle under the stress of the intense heat generated by tons of jet fuel and finally collapse in on themselves sending a toxic cloud of dust, soot, burned metal and human flesh over the landscape, an onrushing lunar fog bearing the stench of death.

The response was an immediate and nearly global expression of grief and solidarity in "America's time of need." For one moment it seemed that the world had come together to condemn what quickly became understood as an act of terrorism, the worst such event in U.S. history.

Unpleasant as it was, America had gotten a taste of an unfamiliar fruit, that of victim.

When the second wave struck, a direct hit by American Airlines flight number 77 on the Pentagon - the iconic symbol of the United States' military power - we were already on a war footing.

Speeches were made and legislation, much of it poorly conceived and hastily drafted, like that creating the Department of Homeland Security, was passed almost unanimously. But slowly the trickle of criticism began. This was especially true upon passage of the Patriot Act [and its first reauthorization] that unfairly maligned body of legislation that provided legal justification for what the country should have already have been doing since at least the Islamist attacks on our African embassies and the USS Cole [1998, midway through the second term of the Clinton presidency] - surveillance of potential terrorist threats. It can be reasonably argued that the increased awareness and intelligence gathering should have commenced upon the 1983 attack on the U.S. Marine barracks in Beirut, Lebanon [first term of the Reagan administration] which killed 241 American servicemen.

Immediately post 9/11 - though it was instantly clear [and therefore not controversial] to the overwhelming majority of citizens that data acquisition and counter-terror operations should necessarily be directed against Muslims with jihadist tendencies - the usual suspects headed to court in order to prevent logic from carrying the day - groups such as the ACLU.

"Four Connecticut librarians who were gagged by the FBI spoke publicly for the first time today at an American Civil Liberties Union news conference about their months-long battle against Patriot Act demands for patrons' library records..."Our clients were gagged by the government at a time when Congress needed to hear their voices the most...This administration has repeatedly shown that it will hide behind the cloak of national security to silence its critics and cover up embarrassing facts. Every time the government invokes national security in defense of secrecy -- as they've done most recently with NSA wiretapping -- the American public should remember these four librarians." [source, Librarians Speak Out for First Time After Being Gagged by Patriot Act, May 30, 2006]

The self-righteous nature of the push-back was typical; though the left had momentarily lost its stride in the wake of 9/11, it quickly recovered and came back, filled with renewed intensity.

> "As a librarian, I believe it is my duty and responsibility to speak out about any infringement to the intellectual freedom of library patrons," said Peter Chase, Director of the Plainville Public Library and Vice-President of Library Connection in Connecticut. "But until today, my own government prevented me from fulfilling that duty."
> [source, *ibid*]

What these politicized government employees were really saying was nonsense, that the Feds had no right to proactively investigate the identities of "patrons" - at free, largely publicly funded institutions - who might have checked out books on how to make bombs and other improvised mass-casualty weapons.

Nearly overnight, America witnessed itself being refashioned from an aggrieved party into an ogreish aggressor, guilty of having the temerity to defend itself against unprovoked attack; the extant political lexicon was being turned on its head.

Hitlerian themes were already being invoked, part of the common parlance as the first massive anti-war protests took place in February 2003, largely underwritten by Marxist organizations like International ANSWER [with suspected foreign funding] a group tied to the avowedly Stalinist, Workers World Party.

The downward spiral continued to gather speed, culminating in 2008 with the presidency of Barack Obama. His middle name, Hussein clearly finding its roots within the tradition of Shia Islam.

In an administration not known for intellectual accomplishment [excepting Cass Sunstein] - it being more the rabid political animal - a former confidante, Rahm Emanuel, team Obama's

Chief of Staff 2008-2010, coined a phrase which captured the sentiments of the left, "never let a good crisis go to waste."

Though a classic technique [think the Reichstag fire and Gulf of Tonkin resolution] for those obsessed with fundamental transformation of society, any kind of crisis - naturally occurring or contrived - presents an opportunity to engage in social manipulation. Sudden threats, to a greater or lesser degree tend, temporarily at least to decouple countries from reality, making citizens more susceptible to ideas and suggestions which would in more normal times never gain a foothold.

The proposition being, radical challenges demand radical solutions, though that is seldom the case in real life.

For those of this mindset, the aftermath of 9/11 was the quintessential opportunity.

It was around this time when a truly bizarre concept - previously latent - was thrust upon an unsuspecting public, Islamophobia. In a few short years it became the de rigueur epithet that the Islamists and their allies employed against critics. Given that Americans had already been directly victimized, labeling them as bigots was a secondary assault.

Consider the nature of the action-alerts/press releases less than 90 days after the horrific attacks issued by the Council on American Islamic Relations. Note the brazenness of CAIR's invective. Its combativeness was buoyed by the lack of a public perception as to the organization's real nature, which became clear in 2007 [as part of post trial proceedings following the U.S. v. Holy Land Foundation conviction] when it was established by the Department of Justice as being associated with the terrorist group HAMAS

> "Since the 9/11 attacks, CAIR consistently has accused the U.S. government of targeting Islam itself in the war on terrorism. CAIR denies the legitimacy of virtually all U.S. antiterrorist efforts and claims that almost every

prosecution or attack on a terrorist who is Muslim, or any investigation or prosecution of an alleged terrorist front group, is an attack on Islam itself." [source, Steven Emerson, CAIR claims that the War on Terrorism is a War on Islam, Investigative Project on Terrorism]

CAIR pressers December 2001:

"After HLF's assets were frozen in December 2001, CAIR issued a joint statement…"We ask that President Bush reconsider what we believe is an unjust and counterproductive move that can only damage America's credibility with Muslims in this country and around the world and could create the impression that there has been a shift from a war on terrorism to an attack on Islam."

And:

"American Muslims are now under a cloud of suspicion produced by a drumbeat of anti-Muslim rhetoric from those who are taking advantage of the 9-11 tragedy to carry out their agenda of silencing our community and its leadership once and for all."

It became impossible to avoid the term as citizens were hammered by a repetitive campaign - media water-torture - that the United States was an inherently bigoted country which had, with no provocation, simply turned against its Muslim minority population.

The textbook definition of Islamophobia is an irrational fear or revulsion of anything which could even inferentially be linked to Islam. That the concept had "legs" in the media sense of the word, absent any empirical evidence, is demonstrative of the damage sustained by American society - PTSD set against accusatory physic violence.

If we stipulate the point for the sake of clarification, that Americans have a certain level of antipathy towards Muslims, it would nonetheless defy logic that such feelings wouldn't be justified...memories of three-thousand ugly deaths welling up.

Observing the spectacle of Muslims figuratively, repeatedly sexually assaulting the nation and then blaming the victim, it would only seem prudent to act in a manner that was at least thoughtfully cautious. There comes a time in which even a public - pop-culturally fixated on the size of Kim Kardashian's ass - understands that it is being guilted regarding a risible canard.

The politically charged word has thus been honed by skilled manipulators to a scary-sharp edge, jihad of the pen often being mightier than that of the sword.

Hard data aside, the constant assurances that that only a spectacularly small number of Muslims are violent flies in the face of reason when the public sees every major American Islamic organization engaged in, as the CAIR poster veritably screamed, an effort to, "Build a Wall of Resistance, Don't Talk to the FBI."

Giving further the lie to the misrepresentation that mainstream American Muslim organizations are genuinely concerned about policing their own communities, why is it that we only find out after the fact that Abu Kareem bin-Ramadingdong has gone bad? Why aren't congregations turning their evil spawn over to law enforcement before they actively join the jihad?

But, but, but...Kareem was such a nice, quiet Muslim boy...

Recent polling information shows that an alarming number of supposedly peaceful American Muslims must be considered within the threat profile.

For example:

> A majority, 51% believe that U.S. Muslims should be able to choose whether they are governed under the Constitution or the Shari'a.

> 29% think that violence is justified against those engaged in "insulting" Mohammed or Islam.

> 25% feel that violence can be used in the United States as part of the global jihad. [source, <u>Poll of U.S. Muslims Reveals Ominous Levels Of Support For Islamic Supremacists' Doctrine of Shariah, Jihad</u>, Center for Security Policy]

So much for the myth of the "teensy-weensy, insignificant" number of American Muslims who might present a problem. With a population of approximately 2.5 million, 600,000 potential domestic jihadis is a bracing image.

Logic, augmented by empirical evidence dictates that one disregard the mythic assertion that American Muslims are in any way engaged or even marginally interested in a campaign of rooting out and turning in their bad players, because distinctly the opposite has and continues to be the case. The active refusal of American Muslims to "clean up their own act," is one of the key indicators that a shell game is in process.

The American public understands the threatening ideology of significant numbers of its minority Muslim population because it inhabits the real world and therefore fails to succumb to the idiocy of the official weasel-word spin-merchants...who call the shots.

Though the "Wall of Resistance" controversy surfaced only 5 years ago, it seamlessly meshes with what has been CAIR's policy from 9/11 onward, resist the efforts by American law enforcement to prevent further Islamic terror attacks by claiming that intelligence gathering is "religious bigotry" by definition.

Muslim name calling is only one tool in the transformational bag of tricks all of which are designed to support allegations of a failed traditional culture while actively subverting it. The creation of linguistic/conceptual constructs as new social levers is an ongoing process.

The remanufacture of language is part of the larger campaign of disinformation. Aside from the stigmatizing effect of being called a bigot or hater, if repeated often enough, groundless accusations enter the common parlance. From there it's a short hop to them being accepted as factually correct by a public which has little technical knowledge to offset the created impression.

For example, the Marxist/progressives have had what amounts to an almost total victory as it has radicalized environmentalism. To a very large extent they now entirely control the narrative. This has been done using the now familiar method of creating an alternate reality, that the West is a despoiler primarily through the agent of capitalism.

The technique can be explained in another way: The left long ago discovered that it's relatively easy to create impressions using bumper-sticker like, emotion based slogans which will be accepted with a high degree of certitude by portions of the electorate, if they're capable of creating a certain amount of ethical resonance. When one becomes emotionally captured by the idea that by mere acquiescence you can seize the moral high ground it makes no difference that these button-pushing assertions lack validity when subjected to the hard light of objective fact.

Though fraudulent, the doctrines which are assembled around spurious declarations become the stuff of zealotry which then are siphoned into official institutions, notably, government schools where all students are now thoroughly inculcated into believing what it demonstrably untrue.

Note: All but a few schools [Hillsdale College being a shining example] from the level of kindergarten to prestigious graduate level centered institutions are indisputably government controlled reeducation centers. The trick is that even if well intentioned, once these teaching factories accept even a single dollar of federal money, they are saddled with whatever the central authority demands.

The hook is set...

A real-world illustration provides a teachable opportunity about how the insidious process of cooptation works as the drones are sent from the hive to work their mischief:

The June 15, 2015 Conde Nast Traveler magazine published an article dealing with outdoor adventures which included the following text:

> "Wolves, it turns out, are integral to the ecological balance of the 3,400-square-mile park. By 1926, the last native wolves had been eradicated in an uninformed and ultimately destructive policy that favored livestock. Without their major predator, the elk herds ballooned and Yellowstone became devastated by overgrazing. The herds even scoured the willows and cottonwoods that grew along the rivers. Then in 1995, in a program initiated by the U.S. Fish and Wildlife Service, the first Canadian gray wolves were reintroduced into the park. Their success and adaptability surprised even the biologists. Packs formed, disseminated, and thrived. [source, Peter Heller, On Safari in Yellowstone National Park, America's Own Serengeti]

Though operating under the title of "nature writer," upon a minimal amount of digging it becomes clear that Mr. Heller is a propagandist pushing the radical environmentalist party line and not merely a humble scribe.

He admits as much on his personal website:

"In December, 2005, on assignment for National Geographic Adventure, he joined the crew of an eco-pirate ship belonging to the radical environmental group the Sea Shepherd Conservation Society as it sailed to Antarctica to hunt down and disrupt the Japanese whaling fleet." [source, Peter Heller]

Actually despite Mr. Heller's assurances to the contrary, it turns out that his claim that wolves are integral to the ecological balance of Yellowstone is garbage. Wolves had been intentionally eradicated in the area because of their negative impact on wildlife, especially the park's elk population and the cattle herds which grazed the land under contract with the BLM.

When people of Heller's mindset captured the government agency which controlled wildlife management of the park in the mid-1990s - the Department of Interior primarily - they reintroduced the grey wolf with devastating effect on both elk and cattle.

Since the wolf's return, the elk population has been reduced by over 75%. In 1994, the year before wolves when breeding pairs of wolves were released there were 19,045 animals in the herd, in 2012, less than 20 years later it had shrunk to 3,915. [see, Rocky Mountain Elk Foundation]

Though many of the animals missing from the current census represent wolf kills, an unknown number - being highly intelligent animals - at least some elk have simply high-tailed it out of the park...however the wolves are at least as smart, working in raiding party like teams they pursued their quarry into the surrounding landscape. Though these canine predators prefer [an evolutionary predisposition] to expend as little energy as possible in hunting down dinner, as the herd thinned, they extended their range considerably.

These green Nazis carried the day pushing a false reality partnered with verbal chicanery, that killing off Yellowstone's elk herds and grazing cattle is "ecological balance." By any standard of reasonable assessment the effort has been a disaster except for the eco-freaks who cleverly leveraged the "saving the world" meme into a fundraising bonanza.

Bottom line?

The only "balance" taking place here was a torrential inflow of money which drove the black ink side of the organization's balance sheet.

The Marxists environmentalist movement buoyed by a 20 year string of success is a constantly evolving, ever more aggressive beast, its crowning achievement being the global warming hoax.

Though unsupported by hard data and actually easily disproven by even the most cursory analysis of ice core samples [showing the amazingly cyclical nature of global temperature changes over a span measured in the hundreds-of-thousand of years] it's now considered among the top concerns of the Obama administration which has forced the Department of Defense to assert the sheer idiocy that the doctrine threatens the future of America. [see, Colleen McCain Nelson, Obama Says Climate Change Endangers National Security, Wall St. Journal]

So complete is the victory that global warming - cum man made climate change now that the bogus theory's dirty laundry has been put on display - nonetheless still looms as a deified concept, a sacralized idiom…a "god-word."

This calculated fraud has been foisted on a public with almost no scientific understanding and apparently even less curiosity about matters it considers boring. Since Western governments now lavishly underwrite the enviro-thugs, climate science and many other disciplines have become Stalinized through a process where only research guaranteed to produce ideologically approved results are funded.

If however the truth manages to leak through the skewing

process then the data points are fudged as to comply with what has become secular scripture.

This is exactly what happened in the most public and far reaching climate data falsification scandal of our time which took place at what was being represented as the sentinel of climatology, East Anglia's Climate Research Unit in Britain:

"If you own any shares in alternative energy companies I should start dumping them NOW. The conspiracy behind the Anthropogenic Global Warming myth (aka AGW; aka ManBearPig) has been suddenly, brutally and quite deliciously exposed after a hacker broke into the computers at the University of East Anglia's Climate Research Unit (aka CRU) and released 61 megabytes of confidential files onto the internet. (Hat tip: Watts Up With That) When you read some of those files - including 1079 emails and 72 documents - you realise just why the boffins at CRU might have preferred to keep them confidential. As Andrew Bolt puts it, this scandal could well be "the greatest in modern science". These alleged emails - supposedly exchanged by some of the most prominent scientists pushing AGW theory - suggest:

Conspiracy, collusion in exaggerating warming data, possibly illegal destruction of embarrassing information, organised resistance to disclosure, manipulation of data, private admissions of flaws in their public claims and much more." [source, James Delingpole, Climategate: the final nail in the coffin of 'Anthropogenic Global Warming'?, Telegraph UK]

The damage done to what was once the prestige of science has led many researchers - even those who had previously accepted the anthropogenic climate model - to conclude that the entire scientific establishment has been "hopelessly compromised."

Yet despite having been proven false - with thousands of incriminating pieces of communication attesting to gross manipulation - the man-made global warming theory has lost none of its vigor. As was the case with Rigoberta Menchu, if an emotionally powerful but nonetheless false narrative has proven to be politically effective in establishing the new hegemon, then truth will invariable be the first casualty.

That science absent truth is the intellectual equivalent of voodoo is of little concern as long as the process continues to rule supreme.

All must bow before the precepts of the state religion, of which the environmental movement is just an especially transparent example of success. And very much as in the case of the Shari'a, disobedience is becoming increasingly dangerous, with some legislators as well as college intellectuals now arguing that denying the theory of global warming should be criminalized.

Lawrence Torcello, who teaches philosophy at the Rochester School of Technology seems quite ready to burn the heretics and apostates at the stake in this version of a modern witch hunt.

> "We have good reason to consider the funding of climate denial to be criminally and morally negligent. The charge of criminal and moral negligence ought to extend to all activities of the climate deniers who receive funding as part of a sustained campaign to undermine the public's understanding of scientific consensus." [source, Lawrence Torcello, PhD, Is misinformation about the climate criminally negligent?, the Conversation]

All of these inventive phrases and concepts are designed around one purpose, to destroy the First Amendment, thus ending dissent.

It's intolerance based upon a self-righteousness that is almost instinctual. People within this camp are fully convinced of their ethical superiority and thus feel justified in proscribing behavior which runs counter to their beliefs.

There is very little difference between such an offense and the religious concept of sin. It's a transgression against an imagined moral order.

People in the West are normally quick to at least give lip service to an expansive definition of tolerance; your liberty is unlimited [within the societal imperative] until it interferes with the identical expression of mine.

On the left and within the Islamist mindset tolerance is a very different animal. Herbert Marcuse, a heavyweight Marxist philosopher from the 50s and 60s defined it as an acceptance of that which doesn't hinder the revolution [precisely mirroring the same thought process behind the notion of "defending" Islam by removing that which impedes its cancerous spread].

> "However, this tolerance cannot be indiscriminate and equal with respect to the contents of expression, neither in word nor in deed; it cannot protect false words and wrong deeds which demonstrate they contradict and counteract the possibilities of liberation..." [source, Herbert Marcuse, A Critique of Pure Tolerance: Repressive Tolerance, p. 88]

Such thinking destroys the concept of equality before the law because clearly individuals are not treated in the same manner...everyone is equal, but some are more equal than others. In this system the purveyors of counter-revolutionary thought, have no right to freely express it.

A political contest within a democracy modeled on Marcuse's type of tolerance wouldn't pit two candidates against each other with the outcome being determined by a vote of the people. It would more closely resemble the type of elections which take place in Iran, where the appointment of approved candidates really negates the necessity of even having the election in the first place, which is merely for show.

Consider the initiative and plot line supporting the ideological precepts of "bullying" and "safe spaces," part of the new stable of fraudulent issues, heretofore without unique, protected class status.

But what really is "bullying?"

It's by design nebulously overbroad and can range from roughing someone up to merely looking askance at a sensitive individual. In the former case what is actually being alleged is assault, a violent criminal act which is already illegal.

What about a disapproving look or scowl?

Has the human spirit changed so radically over the last 100 years that mere disagreement or perturbed glances create mentally anguished parties who must then be provided with special areas - time out "safe space" zones - to protect them from ever being "offended?"

If there's a genuine need for such bizarre creations, doesn't it follow that there should also be a groundswell of support to have "clitorectomy free" safe spaces made available to little American Muslim girls to hide from Shari'a beflaged butchers wielding rusty razor blades intent upon committing an ungodly act? [see, Kristy Kumar, The Underground Epidemic: U.S. Female Genital Mutilation]

Arguably the hottest deconstructionist linguistic/conceptual sledge hammer is the theory of "micro-aggression," which encompasses everything and anything that might hurt the feelings of some transformationally motivated cake-eater.

Acting upon the authority of recently distributed executive "guidance" at the once renown University of California, now run by a nasty piece of work, "Big Sis Napolitano," the term "melting pot" is now off limits, having been judged to be a "micro aggression." Those of non-European descent apparently consider the term defamatory, bristling at the very idea of acculturation...of becoming genuine Americans.

The doctrine of micro-aggression is designed for one thing only, to end freedom of speech. Oddly, the stalwart defenders of First Amendment protection of the indefensible, the ACLU, are nowhere in sight.

Enter speech codes.

> "Speech codes come in many forms. The University of North Dakota bans student speech that "feels offensive" or "demeaning." The University of Missouri at St. Louis boasts a policy restricting speech that will "discredit the student body." Texas' Sam Houston State University broadly prohibits "abusive, indecent, profane or vulgar language." And before it was struck down in federal court this summer, the University of Cincinnati, like many public universities, maintained a wildly unconstitutional "free speech zone." This policy limited all "demonstrations, pickets, and rallies" to an area comprising just 0.1 percent of the university's campus and required all expression in the area to be registered ten working days in advance." [source, Greg Lukianoff, Speech Codes: The Biggest Scandal On College Campuses Today, Forbes]

What about hateful and ugly language that is generally agreed - beyond the insular outposts where Marxism and jihadism run wild - to be over-the-top?

Though we are by no means arguing in favor of speech codes or censoring of expression it must be understood that only the anointed, those who are in ideological lockstep, are permitted to speak with impunity while silencing their opponents.

Let us consider here the most horrific word in the American psyche, regardless of ethnicity - the "N" word - which only Blacks, even mixed-race Blacks, such as the president, can freely use. We of course consider the term abhorrent, but can't help but observe that under no circumstance can these six letters ever cross the lips of a non-Black, unless one wishes to forever live as a social pariah with all that it entails...or worse.

This is by no means a two-way street; whites, conservatives, Christians, heterosexuals and just about anything attached to the tradition of the West are fair game for the most outrageous epithets imaginable, all of which are justified by the left as some sort of payback. Oddly the globe's last bastion of genuine slavery - the Muslim world - is exempt. In this contradictory new environment, indiscreet word choice by a single ethnic group trumps actual, and often brutal, behavior.

The purposeful and obviously pre-planned use of the epithet by the president Obama in a June 2015 podcast was clearly intended to be divisive. He took the occasion to utter the dreaded noun in order to further exacerbate racial tensions in Milwaukee, Ferguson, Baltimore as well as those surrounding the Charleston shootings and the rebel flag controversy. It was Obama and his allies who stoked and further aggravated inter-ethnic enmity and thus kept the race card alive. He skillfully created the meme among dull-witted Democrat clones, that nothing has changed since 1859, the year before the commencement of America's bloodiest conflict, the Civil War - the origin of which was primarily attributable to the viewpoint of an overtly racist Democrat party.

Such is the nature of transformational politics' linguistic manipulation...

In the new Amerikka, certain offenses take on the nature of Original Sin.

No atonement is ever possible, neither blood, national treasure nor good intent will suffice - the stain is indelible and will forever remain unforgivable. That this mindset prevails in a nation with a black president, reelected to a second term and successive Black attorneys general is suggestive of the alternative reality within which DC and its supportive media hive have created.

This, now well established trend is by no means isolated within the confines of the Western world. Orwellianism has gone global especially in the world's numerous flash points such as the Middle East where an ongoing crisis involving a nation that doesn't exist threatens to spill over into a conflict involving all of the major powers.

That place is a make-believe entity, "Palestine."

But how does the Palestinian issue relate to the central core of our thesis?

The simple answer is that it's a near perfect example of how language manipulation, false narratives as well as ethnic and religious bigotry, driven by spiritualized ideologies - in this case Islam - can bring about an astounding cultural and intellectual realignment.

The process has been so effective that thousands of innocents have been killed in its service and a powerless, destitute Arab population has been denied the most basic of human rights - by their own people - simply to make a political point by constantly ripping the scabs off to maintain an open festering wound.

The "Palestinians" have been inculcated from birth into a culture of death, convinced that their plight is due to the "evil" actions of the Israelis and "Zionists" when the truth is that their lives would be far worse absent the largesse and military restraint of the Israeli people. Under the constant bombardment of lies, deceit and indoctrination, the culture is steeped in a suffocating atmosphere where toddlers are given plastic AK-47s and dressed in the colors of HAMAS in preparation for the day when they will have the "opportunity" to become a shahada, a "martyr," dying in some senseless act of terrorism designed only to inflict as much pain as possible while stoking the fires of an endless intifada.

The term Palestinian is in fact a misnomer, historically derived from the word "Palestina," a Roman governorate, so named because it was believed to be associated with the Biblical land of the Philistines.

Let's conduct a thought experiment...

Though the Qur'an is now off limits among the unholy alliance in establishing any linkage between Islam and terrorism, we can't think of a single reason not to take the opposite tack and interpret Biblical history - much of which predates the Islamic holy book by thousands of years - literally.

We refer you to 1 Samuel 17, in which the Israelite champion, a boy...David, faced off against the Philistines' most feared warrior, Goliath who supposedly stood about 3 meters tall. David of course triumphed, placing a well aimed rock from his sling directly between the eyes of the giant, who came crashing to the ground, stone cold dead.

"Now the Philistines gathered their forces for war and assembled at Sokoh in Judah. They pitched camp at Ephes Dammim, between Sokoh and Azekah. Saul and the Israelites assembled and camped in the Valley of Elah and drew up their battle line to meet the Philistines. The Philistines occupied one hill and the Israelites another, with the valley between them. A champion named Goliath, who was from Gath, came out of the Philistine camp..."

Philistines? But, but, but...wither the "Palestinians?"

The fact is that there is, never has been [and never will be] a country called Palestine, nor are there an ethnically distinct group of people who can rightfully claim to be Palestinian. These people are generically tribal Arabs. More specifically they're really squatters in an area more correctly identified as Judea and Samaria. If some kind of [distant] nationality must be bestowed on this area, the West Bank, then it can be thought of as part of ancient Syria or the remnant of the Western part of the Kingdom of Transjordan, an ephemeral state created by the British mandate with no organic basis.

Regardless, the truth is uncomfortable; the territory and people now so commonly referred to, respectively as, Palestine and Palestinian were created specifically to support the concept of Islamic jihadist expansionism.

Not that long ago even fanatical members of Yasser Arafat's murderous Palestinian Liberation Organization [PLO] unblushingly admitted that the concept was simply a political device of convenience.

Former Syrian President, Hafez al-Assad [father of the embattled Bashal al-Assad], dared speak the then non-controversial truth in 1974:

> 'It would be fitting for us to mention to the responsible Israeli authorities that we view Palestine not just as an inseparable part of the Arab nation, but as a part of Southern Syria.' In 1987, he reiterated himself at a conference in Amman, 'A country named 'Palestine' has never existed.' Jordanian King Hussein responded, 'The appearance of the national Palestinian persona serves as a response to Israel's claim that Palestine is Jewish.'" [see, Tsafrir Ronen, Hadrian's Curse - The Invention of Palestine, Part I - The Secret all the Arabs Know, Think Israel]

This is a clear admission that the concept was created specifically to fan the flames stoking the global Islamic jihad.

The candor coming out of Yasser Arafat's PLO was even more remarkable. Given the very nature of its name, there seemed every reason for it to assert the existence of some mythic "Palestinian" entity.

Zuheir Mohsen, a high ranking member of the PLO in the late 1970s, speaking to a Dutch newspaper stated that "Palestine" exists only in the sense that it's politically divisive.

Mohsen's admission at the time stands in stark contrast to the current narrative of a predatory Israeli state; he frankly admits that claiming there are a "Palestinian" people is an ideologically driven fable...shades of Rigoberta Menchu.

"In Between Jordanians, Palestinians, Syrians and Lebanese there are no differences. We are all part of ONE people, the Arab nation. Look, I have family members with Palestinian, Lebanese, Jordanian and Syrian citizenship. We are ONE people. Just for political reasons we carefully underwrite our Palestinian identity. Because it is of national interest for the Arabs to advocate the existence of Palestinians to balance Zionism. Yes, the existence of a separate Palestinian identity exists only for tactical reasons. The establishment of a Palestinian state is a new tool to continue the fight against Israel and for Arab unity.

A separate Palestinian entity needs to fight for the national interest in the then remaining occupied territories. The Jordanian government cannot speak for Palestinians in Israel, Lebanon or Syria. Jordan is a state with specific borders. It cannot lay claim on - for instance - Haifa or Jaffa, while I AM entitled to Haifa, Jaffa, Jerusalem and Beersheba. Jordan can only speak for Jordanians and the Palestinians in Jordan. The Palestinian state would be entitled to represent all Palestinians in the Arab world en elsewhere. Once we have accomplished all of our rights in all of Palestine, we shouldn't postpone the unification of Jordan and Palestine for one second." [source, Wikipedia, Zuheir Mohsen]

The Islamic/globalist effort to carve out a state for a nonexistent people, serves two purposes; it's a rallying cry [a very effective one] to stoke enmity against Israel. It also serves as a unifying ideological force within Dar-al-Islam and the denizens of the West's capitals, not to mention the EU's seat of power, Brussels.

At this point we wouldn't blame the reader for asking the question, what is this, mass insanity? The answer would be, yes in a certain sense there might be psychological elements at work here which are useful in understanding the pathological spread of the new ideology of repression.

Stepping back in history to Europe's Middle Ages we encounter the phenomenon of mass hysteria now called choreomania, then referred to as the "dancing plagues" or St. Vitus' Dance.

Occurring periodically, often in conjunction with the many natural disasters which took place in those bleak times such as the Great Plagues, groups of people would spontaneously break into bouts of uncontrolled, spastic dancing with the participants often screaming and yelling. This would continue for days or even longer, to the point of utter exhaustion and sometimes even death.

An odd aspect of St. Vitus' Dance was that in some cases those who were overwhelmed by the desire to participate in this "danse macabre," seemed to be aware that what they were doing was bizarre but were unable to control themselves. Sometimes they pleaded with onlooking clerics to save them, from what they understood as being demonic possession.

Respected medical journals such Lancet, a magazine published for surgeons, have validated what might seem to many as fanciful folk tales:

"[the historical record speaks] of a bout of unstoppable, and sometimes fatal, dancing in the German town of Erfurt in 1247. Shortly after, 200 people are said to have danced impiously on a bridge over the Moselle River in Maastricht until it collapsed, drowning them all. Likewise, dozens of mediaeval authors recount the terrible compulsion to dance that, in 1374, swept across western

Germany, the Low Countries, and northeastern France. Chronicles agree that thousands of people danced in agony for days or weeks, screaming of terrible visions and imploring priests and monks to save their souls. [John Waller, A Forgotten Plague: Making Sense of Dance Mania, Lancet Magazine]

Of course we aren't suggesting that mania alone as a causational factor explaining induced cultural modification. However, it's especially evocative - in an allegorical sense - in helping one grasp the deeply ingrained motive forces that drive the censorious left. In an almost clinical sense, mass hysterical behavior represents evidence of how malleable culture can be where under the right conditions, irrational behavior can be generated and then transmitted like a virus.

On a different level we see certain parallels between choromania and a process first identified by Dr. Kenneth Levin in his groundbreaking work defining the "Oslo Syndrome" - a condition in which a population under continuous siege and thus tremendous psychic tension can be led to identify with the critique of its oppressors:

> "Segments of populations under chronic siege commonly embrace the indictments of the besiegers, however bigoted and outrageous. They hope that by doing so and reforming accordingly they can assuage the hostility of their tormenters and win relief. This has been an element of the Jewish response to anti-Semitism throughout the history of the Diaspora. The paradigm on the level of individual psychology is the psychodynamics of abused children, who almost invariably blame themselves for their predicament, ascribe it to their being "bad," and nurture fantasies that by becoming "good" they can mollify their abusers and end their torment." [source, Dr. Kenneth Levin, The Psychology of Populations under Chronic Siege, Jerusalem Center for Public Affairs]

Though the subject here is the state of Israel, no culture is immune; after having been subjected to decades of psychological rape, a certain percentage of individuals accept at least a part of their oppressors' critique. Subjected to thousands of years of mistreatment and blood libels at the hands of an anti-Semitism which today is ascendant, some Jews internally ask themselves, "what have I or we done to bring this on?"

The process can lead to widespread social psychosis.

It's not coincidental that after nearly 170 years of Marxist invective, the beneficiaries of capitalism - one of the West's crowning, liberty affirming achievements - are pondering some of the same questions and to a degree responding in a similar manner seeing themselves as defined within the Marxist world view.

Those rolling the loaded dice in this high stakes game of bait and switch have also established fallback positions, as was the case in developing the Gramscian model to account for the failure of the workers to revolt as Marx predicted, also providing cover to Lenin's laughable "clarification" of Marxist dogma, that the inconsistency was due to complications arising from the "division of labor."

Modern techniques using Gramscian theory cut to the heart of the matter; if all else fails and the body politic cannot be sufficiently changed to be receptive to "the revolution," unfettered immigration looms as the ultimate weapon of cultural upheaval.

Flooding the country with illegal immigrants is the transformationalists' fail-safe mechanism to forcibly change the demographic of the United States, over running it with millions of illegal aliens, primarily Mexicans, but lately, of more concern "refugees" from the always war torn Arabic world. These people regardless of their origin aren't dreamers, many are illiterate in their own language, generally unskilled and have zero respect for notions such as enlightened representative democracy.

Once the radical reformers establish "a pathway to citizenship" for these net consumers of social services, the unelected black robed mafia will quickly grant them - via judicial fiat - the right to vote.

At that point traditionalists will have two options, accept a forever ruined America under authoritarian rule or revolt while there's still a chance.

Operations just conducted as of this writing under the code name Jade Helm 15 are clear evidence that the Feds are fully aware of what their social engineering might bring about. Never before in the history of the United States has the Special Operations Command [USSOCOM] engaged in domestic war-gaming. To our knowledge USSOCOM has never undertaken coordinated joint exercises of this nature.

Throughout this section there has been left unsaid a point which must be dealt with. The decrepit understanding by the average American of the basic notion of republican government.

Elemental concepts - liberty, freedom, the need for property rights, the difference between democracy and republicanism as well as understanding how equality of opportunity has nothing to do with equality of outcome, have been scrubbed from the public consciousness under the tutelage of government schools taught by tainted instructors.

In the 1930s George Orwell coined the term "newspeak" in which accepted wisdom was supplanted by the slogans of the new totalitarianism, "peace is war," "freedom is slavery" and "ignorance is strength."

Understandably, many if not most citizens can't differentiate between our form of government and that of a pure democracy, assuming that they are one in the same. Ordinarily this would be of little concern, no one expects the populace to be adept political scientists. However that misses the point; self-rule can't thrive amidst an electorate in which so many can't articulate even a grade-school grasp of basic civics concepts.

Trying to instruct them otherwise is pointless, eyes immediately begin to roll.

Purposefully, the Marxist/progressive vocabulary is strewn with the use of the word democracy and/or references to it because they know the word will, for most, be understood in the common parlance ["democracy" = good] not a technical sense.

But again these aren't common times and the transformationalists understand that their program can be more easily sold if it's wrapped in shiny red, white and blue paper. The intent is clear. These people - whose entire lives are bound within a political philosophy - know that a direct democracy is the perfect tool with which to foment revolution.

It is also a typical example of how language is intentionally abused in order to hide ulterior motives. Really, it's so much more efficient to have voters shackle themselves rather than having to resort to force in the early stages of social upheaval.

An electorate inculcated into the pathological mindset of victimhood - set within a minefield of claimed inequity and class grievance - engenders rage against a fanciful conception of inequality.

Thus, an ignorant public becomes a mob.

Left unchallenged it can be fatal to liberty and freedom because it encourages, as our Founding Fathers feared, the ability of 51% of the population to take away the rights of the other 49%.

For example, James Madison on pure or direct democracy, the formation of majoritarian factions, forced equality of outcome and thus suppression of minority rights:

"From this view of the subject it may be concluded that a

pure democracy, by which I mean a society consisting of a small number of citizens, who assemble and administer the government in person, can admit of no cure for the mischiefs of faction. A common passion or interest will, in almost every case, be felt by a majority of the whole; a communication and concert result from the form of government itself; and there is nothing to check the inducements to sacrifice the weaker party or an obnoxious individual. Hence it is that such democracies have ever been spectacles of turbulence and contention; have ever been found incompatible with personal security or the rights of property; and have in general been as short in their lives as they have been violent in their deaths. Theoretic politicians, who have patronized this species of government, have erroneously supposed that by reducing mankind to a perfect equality in their political rights, they would, at the same time, be perfectly equalized and assimilated in their possessions, their opinions, and their passions." [source James Madison, The Utility of the Union as a Safeguard Against Domestic Faction and Insurrection, Federalist No. 10]

The duplicitous nature of linguistic and conceptual warfare perfectly interfaces with America's obsession with the fleeting and ephemeral nature of a ghost-like pop culture where nothing is fixed. Because the concept of lasting value no longer has meaning, its loss has had a massive impact.

The progressive/Marxists know they have broken the code of Western Civilization. They have the GPS coordinates dialed in and are now engaged in a battlezone-wide Blitzkrieg - much like a mortar attack, the first shot will be long, the next, short but the third will be right down the stovepipe.

A more graphic way of looking at it is the "gang rape" theory of progressive cultural warfare. All of the traditional institutions have simultaneously come under such vicious waves of psychic attack that now weakness, viewed as being provocative, is evident. The leftist social puppeteers know that their hundred year war has come into maximum focus during an unusual period in history in which the quarry is particularly vulnerable, hobbled by a pacifist post-Christian identity.

The safe harbor no longer exists. The effect is cumulative, each sortie leaves the targeted institution more traumatized and less confident.

Among the champions of this process - mostly the denizens of the East and West coast power centers - a nihilistic madness has taken hold. In San Francisco for example in an October, 2016 student election held at the city's Everett Middle School, the Barbie-like Aryan looking blond principal Lena van Haren [a waste by-product of UC Berkeley, naturally] quashed the results because they don't jibe with her vision of diversity.

Of course as is almost always the case in these ideological showdowns, the fact that she is the school's walking anti-diversity poster girl is entirely absent from her consideration.

We find it quite helpful to keep in mind that there is a kind of para-logic inherent in the left's ideological assault of transformation.

On its face the ideology is advanced as a principled, high-minded, self-contained, entirely coherent doctrine intended solely to further "democracy" and "equality" [though it would be unrecognizable as such by the Founders] but looking beneath the shiny exterior surface bubble we see nothing but self-serving ambition, greed and an insatiable, near sexual degree of lust for a slave-like control by people who are totalitarians, organizing the intentionally atomized, alienated masses into foot soldiers in a process where they become agents of their own bondage, a theory central to social philosophy of Hannah Arendt.

> "On the one hand, the police state destroys all relations between men that still remain after the discontinuance of the public-political sphere; on the other hand, it demands that those who have been fully isolated and forsaken by

one another be able to be brought into political actions (although naturally not to genuine political action)...Totalitarian rule does not only rob men of their capacity to act; rather, with inexorable consistency, it makes them - as if they were really only a single man - into accomplices in all action undertaken and crimes committed by the totalitarian regime..." [source, <u>Hannah Arendt: Critical Essays</u>, Edited by Lewis P. Hinchman and Sarah K. Hinchman, p. 217]

CHAPTER EIGHT - THE GUTENBERG DILEMMA: FROM THE ORAL TRADITION TO TWITTER

The near omnipresence of popular culture, communicated through an osmotic mass media, hints at something more elemental - the stark reality against which the "hard copy" world is set. In a strange way we must use the media, which we know induces profound effects of its own, to examine itself.

Though the phrase itself has long been dated, the concept and effect of the "24x7 news cycle" most certainly isn't. Arguably it's the most powerful element in how mankind sees the world while also serving up, as it were, the various components from which individuals form their separate realities. Far more than being the equivalent of last year's 'paradigm shift" with a fresh coat of paint, it's a central issue, which will always to a degree be hazy in resolution.

Indicative of this, we see a failure by many "conservatives" to comprehend the nature of the now, not-so-new world of electronic communication when they limit their counter-offensive to whining about political bias. Though the progressive nature of the press is irrefutable, in the larger sense these folks ignore the ghost of Christmas past which looms scheming behind the curtain.

Inside that shroud lurks the big "M" media, or perhaps the medium, more properly. Unobserved because it's in plain view, is the effect which the technology of communication - the delivery mechanism - brings to the process of altering perception. This is true regardless of what the content might be. It affects everything, including how information consumers approach such transactions.

The Canadian intellectual-cum rumpled media star, Marshall McLuhan, became something of a 60's demi-god upon publishing the penetrating manifesto, "Understanding the

Media," his most well-known examination of the new modalities of communication.

It's hard to believe that the appearance of McLuhan and the rise of the youth counter-culture rebellion weren't somehow interconnected, one a symptom of the phenomenon, the other its decoder.

Feeding into the new information delivery systems - which offered an accelerated, immersive experience - was the pre-existing beat/bohemian sub-culture. It was amplified not only by the Beat poetry of free, dissociative verse but new, dangerous music, the blackest of Black improvisational jazz, Coltrane, Ornette Coleman, Miles Davis and other innovators. Following in short order was white European rock, the Beatles, Stones, the Who leading into Led Zeppelin's sonic-sexual assault in an atmosphere already fueled by psychotropic drugs and the intentionally Dionysian and nihilistic fracturing of traditional societal relationships and long-standing mores which defined the movement.

It shouldn't be surprising, within the new regime, that though much of today's music is so atonal and sonically edgy that it in some respects more resembles traces on an oscilloscope rather than human harmonic compositions, it still retains sufficient information to be interpreted in the same manner [by a decidedly different audience] as previous generations delighted in a Bach violin sonata?

These alternative modes of mass expression - and an openness to them - prepared the way for the appearance of the new Tabula Rosa, McLuhan, explaining the process as it unfolded. It was he who asserted that the impact of the message carrier threatened to dwarf that of its content. He called electronic media, "non-lineal, repetitive, discontinuous...proceeding by analogy instead of sequential argument." [see, Lewis Lapham, Introduction Understanding Media, p. XI]

The new media had the effect of, as Huxley would have put it, "opening the doors of perception" in a unique manner. As a result it now serves as the ultimate arbiter, separating knowledge from that which cannot, has not yet or has been refused the status of certitude, such as it is. Access to 'Net-based information is largely determined by its availability as winnowed through search engines, television's content gate-keepers - producers - and the print world's copy and assignment editors.

Of course the largest 'Net based of these "sieves" is Google - a company notorious for its progressivism and ties to the Obama administration. For example, Eric Schmidt served as CEO of Google for ten years, 2001 to 2011 and is now the Executive Chairman of Alphabet, Google's holding company.

> "During the 2012 campaign, Barack Obama's reelection team had an underappreciated asset: Google's (GOOG) executive chairman, Eric Schmidt. He helped recruit talent, choose technology, and coach the campaign manager, Jim Messina, on the finer points of leading a large organization. "On election night he was in our boiler room in Chicago," says David Plouffe, then a senior White House adviser. Schmidt had a particular affinity for a group of engineers and statisticians tucked away beneath a disco ball in a darkened corner of the office known as "the Cave." The data analytics team, led by 30-year-old Dan Wagner, is credited with producing Obama's surprising 5 million-vote margin of victory." [source, Joshua Green, Google's Eric Schmidt Invests in Obama's Big Data Brains]

The effects of the leftist/Obama/media merger are at times subtle. In doing a Google search for a well known jihadist, the "blind sheikh" and convicted terrorist [spiritual leader and chief strategist of the Egyptian Muslim Brotherhood jihadist franchise, Egyptian Islamic Jihad, Omar Abdel-Rahman] the resulting top pages fail to bring up evidence of his obvious criminality...until the "correct" sequence of characters is entered. Similarly this happens inferentially. Using the key phrase "Egyptian Islamic

Jihad," the first search [as of this writing] result is a <u>Wiki</u> <u>entry</u>...however one which fails to even mention Abdel-Rahman. This happens with such frequency that it's difficult not to view it as evidence of intentionality. Because the hidden subterfuge primarily camouflages lefties, Islamists and others of that ilk it's indicative of either a flawed algorithm [unlikely] or more believably [and this includes Wiki] a desire to conceal the sins of the various protected classes under layers of fluff.

The effect is obvious; reality is distorted allowing bad players to be shielded from scrutiny - solely due to their ideological affiliation - unless the search terms are assembled with scrupulous precision, a difficult task when one isn't exactly sure in advance the extent of the associations being pursued. For example consider the prospect of researching Islamic terrorists, who by intent use aliases as cloaking devices.

The process becomes even more opaque noting that Arabic names must be transliterated into English phonetically and therefore can appear in a withering number of ways. Consider perhaps the most simple case, the many ways in which one can spell something as basic as the name of Islam's prophet: Mohammed, Mohammad, Muhammad, Muhammed, Mohamad, Muhamad, Mohamed, Muhamed, Mihemed, Muhameti, Mahamed, Mahomet, and on and on...

However, when one adds the Arabic nomenclature denoting kinship [often going back several generations] words such as abu, ibn, bin, al, etc., the level of complexity can be mind boggling, only further complicating the process of utilizing already demonstrably politicized search algorithms.

Now, if we think of the Internet as the largest repository of information ever to be created it assumes in many senses the role of the book of common wisdom. When the universal storehouse of information obfuscates and hides knowledge it becomes censorious, preventing or at least stifling access to non-ideologically approved ideas and information.

The real power which accrues to those in charge of running the beast is that they alone have the lockset to the public library.

Though the Internet itself is a relatively new creation [see, ARPANET] the technological innovation which has culminated in the triumph of what is now a thoroughly accepted but nonetheless alternative state of human perception, had its origin millennia ago, in the development of the consonantal form of writing, a way of representing speech through the manipulation of glyphic/pictographic symbols. This was the first revolution of its type, creating a unique technology which packaged information in a way which was independent of the spoken word.

The invention of the alphabet was the gateway to the future; affecting all that followed it. The new symbol rich method of sharing information made possible the assembly of books once the use of paper became commonplace. At first this took place one at a time by hand, often elaborately illustrated - sometimes in candle-lit, monastic silence - and then in mass form made possible by Gutenberg's movable type printing press.

Mechanized printing became the revolutionary tool nonpareil, something few consider today, it being elemental to the fabric of modern human experience.

A profound effect was that it made mass culture possible - some might argue inevitable - since the textual materials were now within the reach of most. This paved the way for further transformations, an homogenizing effect, the Enlightenment, Reformation and eventually the electronic information age.

It's McLuhan who explained that we are so immersed in the swirling movement of data that it cannot but have a radical impact on the way in which we see things. Much like fish, we swim in the waters of a newly perceived set of ordered images, eventually becoming oblivious to its existence unless we are specifically looking for it.

The alphabet freed man from the reliance on and the natural limitations inherent in oral transmission, which had existed since antiquity. Storytelling, though rich in content and often beautiful in an experiential sense, has a limited range. Thus from the old to the new, we transitioned from the spoken word to a representational world. Literacy was thus commensurate with the ability to navigate the rich new universe of signs and symbols, one which could convey ideas in ever more complex form.

Traditionally, since the power of a single voice is limited, the effect is localized and can't impact or threaten the individuality or discreet nature of wider communities - that is, there could be no shared culture outside of that imposed by brute force...Pax Romana.

Individuals living outside the range of the pedant's voice couldn't access the message in its entirety and complexity, except by repetition, one person to another which will always lack full correspondence with the original message.

Post Gutenberg, ideas became available in an almost random access format, if you had an interest in this or that subject it could be obtained in its entirety and independent of personal interaction. If only the general outline of an idea was of importance, the dust jacket might provide it. Skim the introduction and maybe a couple of chapters and the basic theme became clear. This was empowering in a transformative way, knowledge available at a time and place of one's choosing with minimal outside intercession.

This made information portable in a way that led to it becoming trans-national - for the first time in human history a hermetic and complete body of ideas could be shared. In very much the same manner as pushing a button on a drink dispenser, everyone with the means and inclination now had access to the Christian Bible in standardized, inexpensive form.

The effect is still hard to imagine fully some 500 years later, as one teases out all its implications and reverberations. Though it's hard for many people to believe that movable type created the assembly line, as McLuhan contented, there are more than enough similarities to preserve it as an intriguing question.

Of most interest to us in this setting is that these collections of pre-packaged ideas made mass culture possible. People would henceforth be interconnected by the printed word, in McLuhan's terms, a "cool" - analytic and rational, as opposed to emotional - medium.

Blessed with the desire, ability and often the right circumstances one could become a member of a larger intellectual whole. Thus one could metaphorically assume some of the ancient mien of the village elder or chieftain absent proof of original thinking, striking command presence or the sheer physical prowess required to impose one's will.

But books, manuscripts, newspapers and the like were only precursors to electronic transmission, defined by the existence of a radically new carrier with a hypnotic, almost addictive presence.

In the space of a single generation almost everyone became immersed in the "sphere of influence" of a radio, television, computer or hand-held mobile device. Without them we are cut-off from the world. The little smart boxes - our magical image machines - have become the fundamental mode of interaction and provide the background noise, the vibratory beat of the planet.

Try to live without them now...we have become addicted to living in a pig-sty media quagmire from which there is really no reasonable escape outside of the not-so-reassuring understanding that the process is insidious, which might serve in some way to lessen its individual impact.

Remaining literate in the new technologies as they roll out now is vital - USPS mail as a widespread method of interpersonal communication has been dead for some time. Older generations, less inclined to accept the new modalities are cut out of the information loop. As the aged become less and less capable of dealing with this level of change they become casualties of the technology. This can be life threatening since this is now the primary source of communication of a medical nature, access to records, test results, prescription refills, contact with your various physicians; all depend on the ability to manipulate and sometimes assuage [when they become capricious and demand attention] the little mass-produced plastic gods.

Consider how 'Net based systems have improved the delivery of almost all essential services, with microprocessors now commonly seen in everything from automobiles to toasters; everything it seems is now linked within a digital whole. In many ways, though, rather than freeing the individual, these little engines negatively impact liberty and freedom because those who control the flow of information into which all of this data is eventually dumped and integrated know more about our personal behavior than many care to realize or even contemplate

The method of imparting knowledge ingrained within the structure of the modern culture bypasses the circuitry of the human will - it's simply there and impossible to ignore, indicative of its significance. Resistance isn't an option...the new motif is not unlike a universal solvent. Within the oral tradition, dispensation of knowledge was interpersonal, assuming all of the many attributes of a performance, in full-color, visual 3 dimensional texture, sound, resonance and body gestures, all attesting to verifiable reality. The new media however is flat, two dimensional to the point of being cubist as some commentators on McLuhan have observed, where the data is compressed into a series of flattened sharp edges that overwhelm and cut through the senses like a razor. It requires no interpretation because it imposes its own exigencies and like a Picasso, represents an angular, deconstructed entity, a base code not of natural origin.

In this sense, the technology of communication now generates its own content because the wrapper is intermingled with that which it contains.

As with the new music, the oscilloscope trace shimmers.

The emphasis of what constitutes primal information shifts too. Two old saws are amplified here, the sizzle rather than the steak is sold and "if it bleeds it leads" meaning that information of a sensational nature tends to crowd out that which might be genuinely more important but also more prosaic. It is the nature of the medium as it creates shorter attention spans, to have its own bar set higher in order to retain a fickle and jaded audience which it does through an ever increasing level of sensationalism, violence and soft-porn banality, speaking of which, netporn has fundamentally rewired the majority male conception of relationships with women. Perhaps matters wouldn't have progressed in such a direction had it not been predated by the feminist, anti-male movement, perhaps it was inevitable once societal mores became relaxed to the point of non-existence.

As McLuhan summarized:

> "The global village is not created by the motor car or even by the airplane, it's created by instant electronic information movement. The global village is at once as wide as the planet and as small as a little town where everybody is maliciously engaged in poking his nose into everybody else's business. The global village is a world in which you don't necessarily have harmony; you have extreme concern with everybody else's business and much involvement with everyone else's life. It's a sort of Ann Landers column writ large."

In this pixilated world, despite the appearance of almost unlimited choice, a sense of enforced orthodoxy settles in as one has instant access to virtually everything, most of which is of a similar gray hue…500 available channels, but still nothing worth watching.

As early as 1925, Winston Churchill similarly wrote about what he called the "mass effects," understanding that as relationships change between human beings and their surroundings something changes in the relationships between human beings themselves. [source, Winston Churchill, <u>Mass Effects in Modern Life</u>]

Churchill was using his experience in the Sudanese military campaign, especially the "River War," the battle of Omdurman, 1898 to illustrate his contention.

In this battle, the British Army arrayed the periods most deadly weapons - specifically the Maxim machine gun and long range artillery deployed from gunboats - against a vast body of Islamic fighters, some operating under the black flag of the khilafa, the caliphate, who had no understanding of the murderous technology which would soon be put to deadly use against them, often at ranges exceeding half a mile. The Brit's adversaries were armed with muskets of limited range and accuracy which were even then almost museum pieces.

The essay put forth the proposition, with which McLuhan would most likely have agreed, that human relations are deeply affected by changes in technology. Churchill saw the dehumanizing effect of the ability to project force from afar. It removed the individual from the experience, in this case the dust, smoke, din of battle and personal responsibility to act with wisdom and bravery in the face of great danger because of the ability to engage an enemy at ranges far beyond the limits which previous weapons and imagination imposed. To a great degree this is also a demonstration of the principle of the inevitable domination of traditional civilizations by those with superior technologies.

This remoteness from the actual experience induces a kind of estrangement and alienation from what was previously contact which was the epitome of "in your face."

But these powerful changes have already come to pass, are steadily progressing and advancing beyond our ability to gauge the nature of [assuming there is one, a shaky proposition] an endpoint.

Essential questions abound: while it appears that much of

mankind has in part already escaped from the control of individuals in the old sense, aren't our affairs increasingly being governed by mass processes and herd instincts instead? Doesn't it appear that modern information technologies create a climate which discourages what might traditionally be considered outstanding morally sound personalities and their concomitant ability to positively influence events? And lastly and most importantly, will this be for our greater good and glory and reflect well upon us as a species?

These questions merit deeper examination by thoughtful people.

The collision, melding and interplay between these forces will increasingly be the primary driver of an irresistibly evolving Western Civilization. The global affects of which will be vast and more profound than we have space to develop here, as reflected in our decision to simply list some of them below, in no particular order, whereby we trust the reader will be able to more fully consider and explore the implications:

1. Electronic media is inherently subversive and transformational. It tends to overwhelm and sublimate all that has come before it. In the process, consumers have become acclimated to instant obsolescence and have embraced the palliative, transfixing nature of a gossip like alternative reality available at the touch of a button.

2. Since it's largely tradition which is being overturned, it's the maximal social engineering tool. While the amount of content increases at an exponential rate, the information factories - the culture forges - have been subjected to the same Gramscian overturning effect as has the rest of society, with the same result, the left dominates the 'Net.

3. Lest one doubt our previous assertion, let us briefly revisit it. Consider the Google information winnowing algorithm and how even the most innocuous search - but this time one involving a topic or person identified as conservative or a member of the right such as George W.

Bush - almost invariably produces not platitudes but rather a stream of nasty progressive garbage. Often in searches of this nature one must wade through dozens of pages of propaganda to even establish a basic set of facts. 'Net based encyclopedias are another tour de force illustrating the victory of the societal engineers. Thoughtful information consumers who spend any time at all analyzing the political slant of this type of data will be challenged to find unkind words written about the darlings of the left...pssst...Che was a saint.

4. Similarly, in the case of searches directed towards the Muslim Brotherhood, it seems that the top content was assembled and then vetted at Al-Azhar University in Cairo, the world's premier jihad factory.

5. The real power exercised here is unequal treatment of information, aka censorship, the ability to determine that which is "legitimate" and what is not. This is why scumbags like George Soros fund disinformation operations such as Media Matters because its agendized content is presented alongside that of legacy media while the conservative alternative press is with great intentionality, shut out or hidden beneath pages of screeds. Here we speak from direct experience with the Googleplex; these decisions are made by kids who know nothing about the news business, journalism or related matters. And it all plays out within the charged totalitarian atmosphere which shrouds all of Silicon Valley and its hand and glove arrangement with the hard left.

Never in the history of man have so few politically identical individuals made such momentous cultural decisions.

6. Digital communication has supplanted all other forms of message transmission in its immediacy, immersive nature and omnipresence. What appears on the display surface receives a kind of imprimatur, a certification of

verified reality. To many, conversations on Twitter are every bit as real and important as physically communicating with others.

7. The process produces a self-conscious society defined by triviality, the sensational and the banal - one in which people become hyper-sensitized and emotionally frail. The latter is reflected in a faux sense of righteous indignation, an attribute of the new preferred human model, the "caring" person. For many, this misplaced emotion now provides a definitive sense of self-absolution because only those who "care" can be good individuals. It's within this dialectic that the power to label another as a "hater," becomes a prodigious weapon. It's an all weather pejorative designed to silence critics and those who dare opine outside of the state approved ideology, a term which we hope at some point supplants the less confrontational term, politically correct.

8. Those engaged in this castigation fail to understand it as a kind of a self-induced autism, for example, endlessly generated but meaningless gestures such as the "Bring Back our Girls" hashtag Twitter campaign. Operationally, participating in these silly displays are seen as evidence of how deeply one "cares." Within this continuum, it provides absolution from having to face the reality that "our girls" were sold into sex slavery by a particularly vicious group of Nigerian Muslims. In fact, these girls will never be seen again and the Twitterverse doesn't really give a shit – the indulgence having already been "earned."

9. Though hard to fathom for some, in a world of instant communication between people who have never met each other, the new media has in the minds of entirely too many created a craving for fame. What used to be a quest for recognition based upon hard work, scholarship or other societally approved demonstration of worth, has morphed into a desire to simply become famous, thus cutting out the traditional middle-man and going straight for the

trophy. People crave fame out of a desire for self-actualization. They want proof [remember it's on the 'Net so it's true] of their value in a depersonalized world. This also serves to blur the line between being justly famous for a tremendous accomplishment or being infamous for having committed a sociopathic act. Either removes one's anonymity, however brief the period.

10. The phenomenon of instantaneous communication in real time...globalization, the virtual printing presses running at light speed, churns out a morally neutral, anti traditionalist and hence nihilistic multiculture.

11. Barriers are lifted and entre to forbidden information becomes commonplace one of the effects being a general coarsening of the population governed by the lowest possible common denominator as the higher functions of reasoning succumb to the power of the libidinous mammalian brain. Though one might feel guided by rationalism - lessons learned by cause and effect - that increasingly is not the case.

12. As mentioned in the previous chapter, substantial portions of the population have no idea against which foreign power the Revolutionary War was fought, nor do they seem to care; but on the other hand they're thoroughly obsessed with "The Real Housewives of Beverly Hills" and other net-trash which in its totality devalues the worth of a merit-achieved classical base of knowledge.

13. The obvious potential for abuse and manipulation of the public mindset and its component sectors.

14. Diminution of attention spans dictated by information which is constantly changing and in motion, amplified by its ease of access which is osmotic in nature.

15. Creation of data cycles as curiosity about topics is

created, peaks and then dissolves within a model of never ending birth, decay and regeneration.

16. Increasing lack of privacy on one side and on the other, evaporating inhibitions about sharing the most personal of information.

17. Forging of a vast chimera in which binary information becomes interchangeable with reality. The young are crushed when they are un-friended on Facebook or digitally called names, made fun of or anything which might fall within the definition of "cyber-bullying."

18. Feelings and emotions become governing forces, intention alone suffices.

19. A paperless, ineradicable record of activity ensues. Emails, texts, images, search histories, caches, cookies, preferences, all of which are being used by governments and private concerns to build unsettlingly accurate portraits/profiles of behavior.

20. Constantly expanding networks of linkage which are easily abused as ideas, rumors, intentionally damaging misinformation is administered to the populace almost per IV drip.

21. Empowerment of unchecked activists intent upon mob rule.

22. Depersonalization and alienation, a sense of anomie [Munch's "The Scream"]; everything tinted in shades of a similar hue.

23. Suppression of individuality and nuance, elevating the rights of the group over those of the individual - a rejection of one of our most sacred founding principles. This enhances the belief that everything can be

adjudicated in public via a plebiscite where simple majorities can easily be used to crush individual or minority viewpoints. When you see candid videos of what appear to be normal citizens who are quite comfortable supporting propositions "banning" the Bill of Rights or supporting the confiscation of firearms you are witness to the misplaced, but now commonly accepted principle that your neighbor [or all-powerful uncle in DC] is in reality, your keeper.

Though the ideological roots of leftist theory are by necessity cerebral and intellectual, "cold" in McLuhan's nomenclature, in practice it is excessively emotional, "hot" in his parlance. The totalitarian's popular appeal always is to the senses, envy, greed and ultimately rage are stoked making crowds controllable on the model of Pavlov's laboratory animals.

Republicanism can hardly thrive in this kind of an environment; the politics of forced redistribution - of leveling and equality of outcome - are powerful tools in the sowing of discontent which is necessary to sustain pre-revolutionary, internecine societal conflict.

Conservation and traditionalism are the equivalent of cold mediums, imagine the Founding Fathers being limited to expressing the ideal of Constitutionally bound, representative government within Twitter's 140 character limit,. The legal brief of America's revolutionary torch, the Federalist, could never have come into being if strangled within such a format.

Since books no longer seem to matter, even in its original form would the Federalist have been as compelling a document had it been in circulation today?

Not only is the media an indispensable part of the leftist war machine, the latter really couldn't exist without the former.

Now that we have a better understanding of the power inherent in an omnipresent system of communication technologies, it is perhaps easier to understand how the carriers of the message have so fully overwhelmed the ability of citizens to understand the degree that their way of life is being supremely threatened.

The new media/leftist/jihadist complex advances its agenda, employing media-rich, packaged narratives - often based upon single examples - to create the desired. psychic impression.

The recent, but at this point classic narrative maintains that "official" [law enforcement] violence is used to suppress and often kill innocent people of color who though labeled as criminals, are just mimicking the behavior of sainted icons such as Martin Luther King and Malcolm X, thus "proving," to their satisfaction [a very low bar] the existence of white privilege a tell-tale "read" of a diseased society as this meme is contrived.

The power of these is very real, witness the growing sense of cultural shame and self-hatred which is present in the hearts of Westerners…it didn't happen by accident, but rather was conjured up out of whole cloth

A key aspect of the process is the deliberate and clever misuse and redefining of the terminology and the grand narrative used to describe traditional America. Through constant immersion in the data flow of our daily lives, it slowly seeps into our consciousness, supplanting the founding principles. This is the reality in which we swim; this back door approach allows societal malware to permeate nearly every pore in the body. It is designed with knowledge aforethought that the carrier - like the gelatin capsule which contains the medication - will "melt in the mind" leaving only the impression.

The nature of the carrier is to compress the message into a format which is quickly and largely unknowingly metabolized

Though the historical manner of interfacing with new or contradictory information had to contend with the stern gate keeper which is reason, electronic communication largely avoids that check-point. It's so densely laden with emotion that it sublimates everything before it, much like oceans reducing massive outcroppings of rock to the consistency of sand.

Metaphorically that stone is tradition, Western Civilization's organizing principles and hard won lessons, the path that leads us towards "the good." It is the entire cultural edifice which lies in the crosshairs of the Marxist social engineers who largely control these powerful technologies, using them to unwind, deconstruct and then refashion and or repackage reality.

CHAPTER NINE - THE EDUCRATS ARE COMING

The role which educators have played in waging the culture war has been immense as well as purposeful.

Exhibit "A" being Johns Hopkins University [Baltimore, Maryland] which was founded in 1876 with the explicit mission of bringing "European style" education and its principles to the U.S. American educators scoured Europe for leftist educators - those influenced by the German philosophers - to be used as seed material to transform American higher education.

This regardless of the fact that America already had established the bulk of a prestigious secondary education system, the Ivy League Universities, during the 17th and 18th centuries - Harvard [1636] Yale [1701] University of Pennsylvania [1740] Princeton [1746] Columbia [1754] Brown [1764] and Dartmouth [1769].

Yet, despite this impressive base of classical education, the rapidity with which the fundamental ideological makeover – injected into the host and then incubated by the meddling internationalist/interventionist Bund - became ingrained into the professoriate is remarkable. Johns Hopkins became a kind of breeding ground for "progressivism" which argued, much like their siblings do today, that America's organizing principles and intellectual heritage had become outdated. The rationale for moving past the "ancient ways?" New historical conditions require new "instruments" and "tools," which, deciphered, means a larger and more invasive federal government to better serve these perceived needs.

The progressives couldn't believe their good fortune, seizing control of a formerly benevolent, systematized process [12 and often 16 years] of acculturating instruction and transforming it into a revolutionary beast.

We have come for your children...

Thus, across the land, kids were daily hustled off [with the best of parental intentions] into institutions that were becoming little more - and nothing less - than "hate America" factories.

Johns Hopkins quickly produced two important progressive thinkers, John Dewey and Woodrow Wilson, who would later become the 28th occupant of 1600 Pennsylvania Avenue.

As noted within Political Science coursework offered by Hillsdale College dealing specifically with the American Progressive Movement:

> "As a leading Progressive scholar from the 1880s onward, Dewey, who taught mainly at Columbia University, devoted much of his life to redefining the idea of education. His thought was influenced by German philosopher G.W.F. Hegel, and central to it was a denial of objective truth and an embrace of historicism and moral relativism. As such he was critical of the American founding."

To Woodrow Wilson, the founding principles of America were an impediment to his expansive agenda so he reinterpreted them to allow the type of social tinkering he had in mind. He argued that the road map provided by the founders was so flexible that it not only permitted, but required constant reconsideration as to what type of government would best address the problems of any particular historical period. Consistent with his belief that truth was relative, Wilson quipped, "if you want to understand the real Declaration, do not repeat the preface."

In an essay written in 1907, and widely delivered as a speech in public forums, he more fully developed this thesis:

> "We are not bound to adhere to the doctrines held by the signers of the Declaration of Independence. We are as free as they were to make and unmake governments. We are not here to worship men or document. Neither are we here to indulge in a mere rhetorical and uncritical eulogy.

Every Fourth of July should be a time for examining our standards, our purposes, for determining afresh what principles what forms of power we think most likely to affect our safety and happiness that and that alone is the obligation the Declaration lays upon us "

The future president felt this way because he knew that Madison, Jefferson and others who created America's core foundation were mindful of the excesses inherent in large bureaucratic governments and specifically designed a system which internally checked itself to prevent the passions of the masses from becoming transformed into a majoritarian tyranny. Hence the power of government had to be carefully circumscribed, which of course would thwart his plans.

So he and his fellow professors set about using the universities as transmission nodes in spreading the new bureaucratic and oppressive fundamentalism of the need for Leviathan government. Once these institutions tapped into the increasing resources provided by the federal government [the 16th Amendment - the national income tax - was ratified during this period of time, 1913 to be precise] the process became self-perpetuating and the left, being the totalitarians they are, started "weeding out" professors whose ideology differed from theirs, which has now "progressed" to the point that few conservatives remain in the professoriate.

The fact is, this mechanism is no secret to our most mortal enemies among whom are those engaged in spreading jihadist Islam by all means necessary, so they've taken a page from the progressive left [rebranded as "civilization jihad"] creating myths [Islamophobia for example] to both influence language and to tow the culture in a direction of their choosing using the school system as one of their primary disease vectors.

The accusation of being an Islamophobe still carries an extraordinary amount of impact with many individuals despite voluminous evidence produced by the DOJ which disproves the contention that it even exists. We have been writing about this phenomena for many years, please refer to, [CAIR Continues Big Lie Regarding "Hate Crimes" Committed Against Muslims: FBI Stats Prove That Widespread American Islamophobia Is Nonexistent, PipeLineNews.org, October 12, 2010]

As alluded to previously, central to the process of manipulating culture is the power of the fallacious narrative [the chief export of today's university system] which just happens to be the Marxist deconstructive tool of first resort. As such, it's a curious thing; think of it as a parable which suggests or is presented to "prove" one or more contentions which are inimical to Western principles and indeed have no basis in fact. More technically this happens through a reductive process which rips to pieces that which is being analyzed. This is done because it destroys the bonds and linkages which knit a world view together. The end process results in non-reality becoming indistinguishable from that which is real because all the road signs have been stolen.

That a contention is demonstrably false doesn't detract from its power to influence since it recapitulates Goebbels' use of the "big lie narrative" endlessly repeated as the nation's youth are processed through the assembly line of an aggressively malicious American educational system.

Simply because lies are held as Gospel by many doesn't make them truthful in an empirical sense. On an elemental level it's the illogic of reasoning general points from an example of one, or for that matter something manufactured out of thin air. Despite the fact that the story-lines associated with these cultural "sins" are so broad and unsupported by anything approaching certitude, they are offered as established working theories.

As the philosopher Karl Popper argued, a theory which can't be proven false is unscientific and thus has little merit, it's at best an opinion and cultural narratives fall into this class of rhetoric.

Regardless of how many examples suggest that the assumption is wrong, it continues to maintain its intellectual vigor among the transformationalists. It's assumed to be genuine...true because it's true. At its core the process itself is as unreasonable as expecting that a man can be reconstructed from his cremated remains. Certainly the ashes represent in some sense his essence, but analyzing them will never lead to any real understanding of the being which no longer exists.

As social philosopher Allan Bloom wrote nearly 30 years ago remarking about the role that the educational system has had in building the idealized citizen:

> "We began [with the traditional]...model of the rational and industrious man, who was honest, respected the laws, and was dedicated to his family...Above all he was to know the rights doctrine; the Constitution which embodied it, and American history which presented and celebrated the founding of a nation...The recent education of openness has rejected all of that. It pays no attention to natural rights or the historical origins of our regime, which are now thought to have been essentially flawed and regressive. It is progressive and forward thinking. It does not demand fundamental agreement or the abandonment of old or new beliefs in favor of the natural ones...There is no enemy other than the man who is not open to everything. But when there are no shared goals or vision of the public good, is the social contract any longer possible?" [source, Bloom, The Closing of the American Mind, p. 26-27]

We look to the utopian liberal social philosopher John Rawls to illustrate Bloom's contention.

In Rawls,' A Theory of Justice [1971, as revised in 1999], the author argues that a society based upon the classical theory of natural rights - the pure form of liberty which guarantees equality of opportunity but not equality of result - is unjust, he writes:

> "For one thing, even if it works to perfection in eliminating the influence of social contingencies, it still

permits the distribution of wealth and income to be determined by the natural distribution of abilities and talents..." p. 64

Rawls was [deceased 2002] an academic heavy-weight [Harvard and Oxford] and his most important work - which followed the tumultuous sixties by just a few years - is still used to defend the way the new social order has subsequently been mechanically integrated into the West.

A central aspect of this is a justification of cultural Marxism. As noted in the above cited work as well as his 2001, A Theory of Justice, Justice as Fairness, Rawls champions multiculturalism as an essential aspect of pluralism and "fairness" - in reality a recapitulation of the now age-old Marxist proposition, "From each according to his ability, to each according to his needs" - as democratic justice. The social schemes which he embraced are designed to level-out or mitigate the natural effect whereby those who are brighter, more industrious and make better decisions obtain a disproportionate share of societies' goods and services - which Rawls believes to be inequitable.

Stepping outside of academia for perspective, we present a fairly timely example of the way this revisionism, the desire to reject historically important American values - being open to believing just about anything - works in the real world, this one taken from the combative arena of presidential politics.

During the 2012 presidential election, Mitt Romney, the GOP candidate, was a genuinely decent and deeply religious man, who had made a small fortune on Wall Street as a "turnaround" expert. His group [Bain Capital] identified companies which were failing but seemed to have potential, then purchased and reorganized them hoping to make a profit upon their resale.

An inauthentic thesis was developed by the Obama campaign, one designed to play into the pre-existing and popularly held contempt for the wealthy, especially those who make a living in the financial services industry - you know - those who "really don't work" or "produce anything of value," having no grime under their manicured fingernails. Romney thus became associated with the caricatured "Robber Barons" [a brilliant creation of New York political cartoonist Thomas Nast in the mid 19th century] who were evil, almost invariably white, male, money grubbing heartless bastards who turned orphans and widows out on the street just to make a buck, or sometimes just for the sport of it.

Notwithstanding that the portrait was outlandish, millions accepted it, a priori. An advertising campaign was constructed around the prejudice where a central casting "factory worker" in one of companies which Mitt's corporation held, made the outrageous claim that candidate Romney had killed his wife, denying her medical coverage [which she had obtained through her husband who had allegedly been fired] thus allowing cancer to overwhelm her. The entire presentation was a lie, one which even news organizations as terminally dense as CNN had already debunked. Nonetheless, it served to personalize and justify the big picture that Romney was so ruthless and greedy that the mere killing of a woman wouldn't deter him from working his depraved magic.

That the ads played into the hysteria associated with the Marxist Occupy Wall Street movement [see our coverage, William Mayer, Occupy Oakland October 19, 2011, Taste The Madness] as well as the controversy surrounding ObamaCare only served to make it more timely and effective.

In another illustration of destructive myth-making, one to which we have previously referred, deals with the allegation that American Muslims face massive discrimination. Irrespective of the fact that it's a false allegation, it remains on the lips of Islamists such as Ibrahim [formerly, Douglas, a convert to Islam] Hooper, National Spokesman for the HAMAS linked organization CAIR.

And it's there for a reason…

156

So powerful are these well-told and endlessly propagated fabrications that it has resulted in a widespread mania within the formerly spit-and-polish world of the Department of Defense which has actively worked to purge and suppress supposedly "Muslim hating" instructors and related educational material from its anti-terrorism course work. This undoubtedly has major negative implications for a society under attack by disciples of Allah, who are, if one reads the legacy media, now the victims of a hopelessly bigoted nation.

The number of similar examples in which this technique has been employed is nearly endless:

1. The mindless procedures developed by the TSA post 911, which make no effort to sort out those who most likely don't pose a threat from people who fit the behavioral pattern [portrait] of a terrorist - the model the Israeli's have successfully been using for many years. Uninfluenced by the dementia of multiculturalism, the Israeli pre-flight screening process includes vehicle searches, surveillance cameras placed everywhere, interviews with prospective passengers the length of which is determined by how they respond as well as making religion a consideration. This isn't blind profiling, it's taking every aspect of an individual into account in order to make a judgment based upon decades of experience.

2. The Al Sharpton/Tawana Brawley hoax, and his subsequent and quite costly defamation trial and conviction.

3. President Obama's reprehensible jury tampering in the Trayvon Martin case in furthering a false narrative even after the jury had found the killing justifiable, "You know...I said that this could have been my son. Another way of saying that is Trayvon Martin could have been me 35 years ago. And when you think about why, in the African American community at least, there's a lot of pain

around what happened here, I think it's important to recognize that the African American community is looking at this issue through a set of experiences and a history that doesn't go away." [source, WH website, President's comments regarding the death of Trayvon Martin]

4. The urban myth of a "rape friendly" University of Virginia campus, which we now know was untrue, to the degree that even the comic book periodical Rolling Stone was forced to retract its story on the matter, as it prepares to deal with the ensuing litigation to be brought by those directly affected by magazine's inexcusable libelous assertions.

5. Similarly we note the fallacious allegations in the Duke Lacrosse case.

6. Perverse "diversity" training programs in the military, largely at the behest of President Obama. These programs have been accompanied by a reckless purging of a whole generation of flag officers whom the CIC has judged to be irreconcilable opponents of his manipulation...think, Hitler's purging of the SS, the "Night of the Long Knives" [mid-summer 1934] which helped him solidify power

But as one will note within the president's Martin statement, the facts are irrelevant, with the text having been massaged to serve a larger purpose.

Regarding the defamation of the University of Virginia, the left won't let go of the broader meme lurking behind it. The power of an admittedly false narrative remains because..."well it happens all over, just trust us on this; the capitalist, Muslim hating, homophobic, white privilege, right-wing etc., culture is rotten to the core and must be brought down."

Sadly, this is the essential core of modern "journalism" as it's taught today in America's most prestigious institutions of higher learning. At its core, journalism today largely consists of propagating tall tales which serve the transformationalists. Expanding on this slightly we can absolutely assure you that there is massive cooperation between the leftist/Islamist alliance and the press. Story lines are suggested and shopped, conference calls are held where activists interact with reporters and completed articles are often sent back to whatever organization or group is being promoted and/or serviced, for approval even before the story is submitted to the author's editor. This is not an idle claim, there are thousands of documents, emails especially between activists and journos, that absolutely prove the allegation. Those who claim there is no leftist bias in the media are either idiots or liars. Everyone involved in the business knows it, though few will admit that it's true. There's a logical reason for this: confirmation of the already widely-held belief that the media is strongly biased to the left would inevitably result in the crumbling of the last shards of the profession's credibility.

If you have any doubts about the foregoing we suggest that your peruse Elizabeth Stoker Bruenig's psychotic analysis in the New Republic, <u>Rolling Stone's Rape Article Failed Because It Used Rightwing Tactics to Make a Leftist Point.</u>

> "…Sabrina Rubin Erdely, the investigative journalist and true-crime writer who penned the essay, set out with an answer in search of a question, a conclusion about systematic indifference to rape which she needed the right story to backfill. If she had written a fictional account of a rape that met all her article's needs, I can't imagine it would have been too different than the horrifying one that issued from Jackie, which should have set off alarm bells then…"

A "true crime reporter" who seemingly plays fast and loose with the facts or worse, fails to adequately vet the statements of those making the allegations? This is emblematic of a dogmatic, subversive ideology held with a rigor that would do Ayman al-

Zawahiri proud, either that or Ms. Bruenig should consider buying a ticket to Vienna.

Practitioners of these spiritualized ideologies, as Babbit called them, feel duty bound to observe the prime directive - furthering the revolution. Working towards that goal is all consuming, and we must assume, somewhat fulfilling perhaps in the same sense that a Catholic would feel having completed a Novena or a Muslim making the hajj.

As used by Ms. Bruenig, the technique of reasoning with the conclusion already assumed is exemplary of the aforementioned Marxist technique of "structural analysis." The target is identified, isolated and then killed by fragmenting it into a set of components which though they bear little resemblance to reality, can nonetheless be re-arranged to confirm the critique. We find it instructive that within Ms. B's defense of the indefensible she actually incorporates the term, "structural" so it stands to reason that she might be conversant with the cultural Marxism which serves as a wrapper for the methodology. That there is great similarity between this vivisectionist attack on the West and the techniques taught by Saul Alinsky shouldn't be overlooked. This is entirely understandable since there's nearly a 100% concordance as to intent and principles involved between the two.

Thus, bigotry is proven upon its mere assertion ["we know the U.S. is a racist society because it is"]. The process is rationally tautological only within the confines of that particular belief system's dialectic because from the outside it's obviously ludicrous. Broad societal indictments of our way of life are the analogue of the self-criticism sessions which widely took place in the Soviet Union and Mao's Red China. It's a way of shaming people into the new orthodoxy by forced confessions of not being totally committed to the cause or of failing to have measured up to some, often evanescent, standard.

This is why Rigoberta Menchu's gut wrenchingly untrue tale still retains great vibrancy within the edutocracy and anti-

Western/anti-capitalist bund despite it having been proven fraudulent. These kabuki dances serve a political god who demands absolute loyalty. Any method of arriving there is acceptable despite it creating a trail littered by ruined lives and reputations.

These are the kind of individuals that progressive education creates, mendacious, soulless creatures whose only intent is to re-program the public into accepting the counter-culture's explanation of its false reality.

All of these examples demonstrate just how radically the culture has been, with great forethought, turned on its head. The fraudulent new world we've seen constructed around us has been designed to preclude efforts to reverse the process.

If you oppose the increasing frequency of instances where the American judiciary is deferring to the Shari'a, you are by definition a Muslim hater. If you take issue with gay marriage upon the very reasonable belief that "marriage" as an historic institution has been for thousands of years unquestionably defined as a union between man and woman, you're homophobic. If you believe that the efforts of the Department of Justice and the national security apparatus should be directed against individuals and organizations whose ideology screams jihad, you're a bigot. If you object to any of the attributes of the new order a suitable adjective will be used to culturally shame and ostracize you.

Perhaps, though, it will take a more direct approach...a knock on the door from the IRS or maybe the ancestral farm will be adjudged by the EPA - in an act of administrative thievery - to be wetlands and thus effectively seized without compensation or anything resembling due process.

CHAPTER TEN - CULTURAL DEFENSE RULED ILLEGAL

Ideally - especially in today's environment where authentic mujaheed are carrying out acts of Islamic terrorism on American streets - prudent law enforcement, intelligence practices and legislation designed to protect the security of the nation would be affirmed by the judiciary against the challenges which naturally occur when individuals and organizations intent upon overturning the society petition the courts for relief against those measures.

But these are far from normal times.

We live in a post-constitutional, pre-revolutionary age created by the factors discussed in previous chapters. Courtesy of anarchists, the Islamists and progressive/Marxists, an intellectually sophisticated war - redefining the culture through manipulation of its component parts - is being waged against everything for which the West stands.

As a result, defenders of the historic order find only a querulous sympathy within the justice system, it having been compromised in the same manner as have other social institutions. This is as planned, with words and concepts twisted to the point where self-defense of an aggrieved culture inexorably proceeds towards becoming illegal as the system is turned in upon itself.

The courts have in some large part been captured by the enemy, used to establish new and entirely arbitrary standards of conformity which are then pressed into action with the intent and very real effect of suppressing criticism. In the case of Islam, this transubstantiated jurisprudence becomes an agent of Shari'a enforcement.

The technique itself has a name - lawfare - a many-headed tool of insurgency directed against the culture and conducted within the setting of the American court system. [please refer to The Lawfare Project].

"under successive administrations of both parties, America's civilian, intelligence, and military elites too often have focused single-mindedly on the kinetic terror tactics...but ignored the overarching supremacist ideology of Shariah that animates [them]..Shocking evidence of where such willful blindness or submission leads can be found in Europe. A number of European nations have permitted an unprecedented incursion of Shariah into their courts...there are some eighty-seven Shariah courts that operate side-by-side with English Common Law courts...The problem...is that Muslim women and children may not be able to opt out of Shariah jurisprudence. They are thus subject to grave injustices...effectively creating a second-class citizenry operating under a fundamentally unfair legal system. Many Americans remain woefully unaware of this trend abroad, let alone its emergence here...In 2011, the Center for Security Policy published a ground-breaking study entitled, Shariah and American State Courts: An Assessment of State Appellate Court Cases. For the first time, the entry of Islamic Law into the U.S. legal system at the state court level was documented with a sampling of 50 instances drawn from published appellate legal cases in which an attempt was made to invoke Shariah. These findings confirmed what previously had been only anecdotal accounts, and exposed the grim reality that Muslim American families, mostly women and children, are in very real danger of coming face to face - in America - with the cruel and discriminatory provisions of the Shariah from which many of them had fled in their own homelands." [source, Shariah in American Courts, Center for Security Policy]

Actually, because of the vagaries of the way judicial opinions are filed and archived, those who have examined the matter have little doubt that these 50 cases represent but a small fraction of the numerous instances where Shari'a has influenced the American legal system, with the example of Europe pointing the way.

Doubters need only weigh the issue against the strategy of the Muslim Brotherhood's plan of internal subversion, which has fully absorbed the long-standing leftist strategy of forcing Western democracies into "sabotaging its miserable house by its own hand."

More specifically, the threats from this avenue of attack can be categorized:

1. Decisions ruling against the taking of necessary precautions - such as the methods developed by the Israelis for air travel safety, which has a sterling, empirically unassailable 30 year record of efficacy - to prevent mass casualty attacks, deciding instead that these reasonable policies violate the U.S. Constitution, thus having the effect of making it illegal to take adequate and reasonable measures to ensure national security.

2. Allowing foreign legal concepts, specifically the Shari'a, to bleed into the American justice system, as has been the case in Europe where the infection is more advanced. This is especially true when evaluating the 85-100 Shari'a courts which operate in the UK and the Continent's hate speech codes, which have a dual purpose, serving as agents of Shari'a enforcement while suppressing dissent.

3. A general, overly deferential treatment of all things Muslim, upon the deceitful assertion that actions - though motivated solely by a political ideology - are shielded under the First Amendment's protection of religious freedom.

4. Legal decisions which empower regulatory agencies, often via their rule-making authority, to forcibly change traditional America by fiat.

It bears repeating that Islam, as practiced contemporaneously and normatively is overwhelmingly a political doctrine. As an "ism," it calls for the violent as well as pre-violent expansion [kinetic jihad and its sly cousin, stealth or jihadistic cultural subversion] of a belief system cobbled together in Frankenstein manner by a delusional "prophet" so that "Allah's religion" reigns supreme over all lands, deserves no protection under U.S. law.

Both theoretically as well as in a practical sense, Islam is a creed of dominion, requiring the kufr world [that of the unbelievers, those residing in Dar-al-Harb, the House of War] to humbly submit or face the sword.

No lesser authority than Osama bin-Laden distilled modern Islam in the space of a single paragraph.

> "I am one of the servants of Allah. We do our duty of fighting for the sake of the religion of Allah. It is also our duty to send a call to all the people of the world to enjoy this great light and to embrace Islam and experience the happiness in Islam. Our primary mission is nothing but the furthering of this religion." [source, John Miller, Interview of Osama bin-Laden, May 1998, ABC News as published by PBS]

To illustrate the contention that cultural defense is facing ever increasing legal hurdles there is probably no better example than the case of the "Flying Imams."

This story, now almost a decade old, offers concrete proof of the serious nature of the so far, effective attack on our institutions, freedoms and liberty itself by spiritual-like transformational ideologies. It's the stone-cold face of "civilization jihad," and one would be remiss not to be concerned.

The executive summary of the incident is straightforward:

> "Muslim religious leaders removed from a Minneapolis flight...[having engaged in] behavior associated with a

security probe by terrorists and were not merely engaged in prayers...Witnesses said three of the imams were praying loudly in the concourse and repeatedly shouted "Allah" when passengers were called for boarding US Airways Flight 300 to Phoenix. Passengers and flight attendants told law-enforcement officials the imams switched from their assigned seats to a pattern associated with the September 11 terrorist attacks and also found in probes of U.S. security since the attacks — two in the front row first-class, two in the middle of the plane on the exit aisle and two in the rear of the cabin..." [source, How The Imams Terrorized An Airliner, Washington Times, November 28, 2006]

Left almost entirely unreported was the fact that the imams were returning from a weekend conference of the North American Imams Federation where they were specifically being trained in strategies of media manipulation. [view the NAIF 2006 brochure, 2006 North American Imams Federation Convention, Minneapolis]

The imams involved in this effort designed it as an experiment in how far they might be able to push the cultural jihad model. Criticism of their actions was framed as religious discrimination and bigotry so it's not surprising in the least that Muslim Representative Keith Ellison [D-MN, a speaker at the NAIF conference] injected himself into this matter to provide a faux kind of gravitas, since Ellison is a Congressional nobody who punches well below his weight.

The goal of the plan was simple, to legally and through propaganda, batter the airline and the airport's security team into submission through fear of financial liability. Towards that end the imams operated straight out of the conference handbook describing how to take pro-active action.

"Islam is now almost constantly on the news, and Imams must be capable of dealing effectively with the media. Good communication skills encompass being able to respond to media inquires, fielding questions from journalists, addressing information about Islam and the media, generating positive story ideas, and writing letters to the editor when necessary. Communication should not be limited to responding to misconceptions, but Imams should also take advantage of opportunities to highlight activities in local mosques and the contribution of Muslims to local communities." [source, Beila Rabinowitz, William Mayer, Imam's Minneapolis Airport Stunt - Cultural Jihad, PipeLineNews.org]

Judged by their actions, the imams were waging psychological warfare - cultural jihad. Make no mistake about the operation, it was an entirely political act calculated to globally degrade American airport security by linking the taking of reasonable precautions with anti-Muslim bigotry.

At the time, the question remained as to whether U.S. Airways would hold its ground and resist the gambit. This writer counseled a counter-offensive including a refusal to meet with the imams, their representatives and Congressman Ellison - who saw in the controversy an opportunity to use his newly acquired political clout to promote the Islamist agenda. It was also suggested that the Department of Justice investigate the incident as a conspiracy intended to destroy reasonable and prudent airport security measures, thus enabling future airline based terrorist activities.

But the spineless GW Bush administration simply didn't want to go there...we beg the reader's indulgence here for the following brief, but necessary digression. Though it can't be explored in the depth which it deserves here, the timorous nature of the GWB Justice Department can in large part be explained by the fact that Team Bush had been penetrated by agents of the Muslim Brotherhood, for example Abdurahman Alamoudi, later convicted and sentenced to 23 years as an al-Qaeda financier, who might as well serve as the poster-child of civilization jihad.

As the Center for Security Policy details in, <u>Abdurahman Alamoudi, the Boston bombers, Grover Norquist, and the GOP</u>:

"Alamoudi ran, directed, founded or funded at least 15 Muslim political-action and charitable groups that have taken over the public voice of Islamic Americans. Through a mix of civil-rights complaints, Old Left-style political coalitions and sheer persistence, Alamoudi helped inch the image of U.S.-based Islamists toward the political mainstream and induced politicians to embrace his organizations. He sought to secure the support first of the Clinton administration in seeking to repeal certain antiterrorist laws, but when Bill Clinton failed to deliver, Alamoudi defected to Bush, then governor of Texas. Alamoudi and other Muslim leaders met with Bush in Austin in July [2000], offering to support his bid for the White House in exchange for Bush's commitment to repeal certain antiterrorist laws."

Due to overwhelming pressure, lack of an aggressive offense and above all the failure of DOJ to even lift a finger, the air carrier eventually was forced to cave but in retrospect it's clear that under the cultural realities present even back then, it was problematic that anything [aside from full scale involvement by the Attorney General] could have affected the outcome.

A civil case was initiated [using attorneys supplied by the <u>Council on American Islamic Relations</u>], went to trial and was shockingly decided on behalf of the plaintiffs, the six bellicose imams. A settlement was reached out of court, the dimensions of which remain sealed. Though it has been speculated that only a token amount of money was involved, the establishment of the precedent in case law continues to loom large.

It's clear that the overall strategic goal of this and similar incidents is to take advantage of the malleability of American culture and it was in this manner that the United States - in the instant case as well as others in the same genre - has been prevented, by a skewed interpretation of its own legal codes, from defending itself.

In such a toxic environment, the U.S. Constitution does indeed become a suicide pact.

This is a frightening case, demonstrating that the power of transformational ideologies based upon the Gramscian model have proven quite effective in practice. Perhaps of greater import, it's demonstrable proof that our culture has already been damaged and placed in peril, having permitted itself to be sodomized by Islamist and Marxist thugs and their hired guns.

Unfortunately the intervening years have not been kind to American traditionalism, to wit the U.S. Supreme Court's recent 8-1 decision in - U.S. EEOC v. Abercrombie & Fitch Stores Inc.

The brief of the controversy was that a prestigious clothing merchandiser, Abercrombie & Fitch, refused to hire Samantha Elauf, a Muslima, because she insisted on wearing hijab while on the job which the defendant alleged conflicted with the store's long-established dress code.

The defects of the shockingly lopsided ruling seem obvious. Further darkening the picture was the fact that - as wasn't the case in the Flying imam case - Barack Obama's out of control - get whitey - Equal Employment Opportunity Commission was the party bringing suit on behalf of Ms. Elauf.

1. The decision seeks to speak authoritatively, based upon facts not in evidence, specifically regarding what constitute a "religious" obligation for Muslim women.

2. It negligently expands employment discrimination law to the point where retailers have now apparently lost the ability to present the type of cohesive, positive corporate image the public has come to expect from high-end merchandisers. It incorrectly applies the relevant

legislative language regarding the matter and leaves retailers at increased risk for Islamist blackmail in the form of lawfare.

As stated in the decision's syllabus, the plaintiff sued alleging religious discrimination, "…because the headscarf that she wore pursuant to her religious obligations conflicted with Abercrombie's employee dress policy."

However, contravening what the 8 amateur imams in the Supreme Court majority determined, there is no Qur'anic basis upon which to support the claim that wearing hijab is a religious requirement for Muslim women. The most relevant passage simply stresses the need for women to dress modestly, something common to both Christianity and Judaism - another example of the way in which Mohammed pilfered pre-existing theology to "flesh out" his "hybridized" political ideology, Islam.

> "Tell thy wives and thy daughters, as well as all [other] believing women, that they should draw over themselves some of their outer garments [when in public] this will be more conducive to their being recognized [as decent women]…" [source, Qur'an, Al Ahzab,/Sura 33:59]

Thus wearing of the headscarf is at best a cultural affectation [and thus, upon that basis alone, inappropriate in a Western setting] and can hardly be considered a requirement consistent with being a devout Muslim woman. Therefore Abercrombie appears to simply have been enforcing its "neutral look" policy which is religiously neutral in its reading and practice.

The sole dissent was written by Justice Thomas, who quickly cut to the heart of the matter…the court was, once again, writing rather than interpreting law.

> "Resisting this straightforward application of §1981a, the majority expands the meaning of "intentional discrimination" to include a refusal to give a religious applicant "favored treatment." But contrary to the

majority's assumption, this novel theory of discrimination is not commanded by the relevant statutory text..."

As Thomas further stated, "[the finding] creates in its stead an entirely new form of liability: the disparate-treatment-based-on-equal-treatment. Because I do not think that Congress' 1972 re definition of "religion" also redefined "intentional discrimination, " I would affirm the judgment of the Tenth Circuit [ruling against plaintiff] I respectfully dissent .."

Aside from the establishing, entirely without basis, of another incomprehensible standard regarding employment law, the majority seems to have, in its haste to cater to current popular trends, given no thought whatsoever to the idea that by deciding this matter in favor of the EEOC it has transformed the Supreme Court of the United States into an agent of Shari'a enforcement which we consider violative of the establishment clause of the First Amendment.

The incongruity of a finding of "disparate treatment," based upon admittedly "equal treatment" is demonstrative of the degree to which even so-called conservative justices have expanded the power of an authority from which there is no appeal. Furthermore the decision will have the effect of intimidating employers against taking any actions which might in any way offend what is certainly the most litigious group within America, its perpetually cranky Muslim population.

If this ruling is taken to its logical end, then Abercrombie & Fitch could have been found guilty of not hiring an applicant dressed in a burka, an absolute requirement within the Salafist sect of Sunni Islam. Taken to the point of absurdity, where does this end, are we to believe that Muslim retailers selling halal food will be forced to hire Hasidic Jews dressed in traditional black garb and sporting payot [sidelocks]?

No, though the Supreme Court has widened the street beyond reason, it remains implicit that traffic is only allowed to move in one direction - towards "accommodation" with those whose intent is eventually abolish the high court, replacing it with one making determinations based on the Shari'a - a Shura Council. Ironically, such a body would have far great ideological consistency than does the current SCOTUS...twisted though they are, jihadis at least have principles.

Being of such recent vintage, and considering the lopsided nature of the vote, the Abercrombie & Fitch case was and remains a particularly impressive win for the above-ground jihadists and a very sad day for those who seek to preserve the intellectual and legal heritage of the West. This is a classic case of lawfare and should give every American - regardless of religious affiliation, or lack thereof - pause for great concern as once again a court, in this case the highest in the land, legislated from the bench, allowing the enemy to further subvert the culture. As a commentary on where the country stands in the battle to effect a soft revolution, we find it unremarkable that the issue of an American court acting as an agent of Shari'a enforcement was never mentioned in the legacy media.

Moving on, the recently decided Supreme Court case [5-4] described below provides evidence of how the abusive use of governmental findings of "discrimination" and other supposed offenses where they don't exist, limits the right of citizens to defend the culture they in part create when doing as simple as choosing where to live.

The problem as the Department of Housing and Urban Development [HUD], the Equal Employment Opportunity Commission [EEOC] and the rest of the federal government sees it, is that the real-world demographic distribution of various "protected classes" throughout the United States is unacceptable because the composition of every community isn't identical to that of the bureaucrat's idealized diversity model.

The decision, Texas Department of Housing and Community Affairs et al. v. Inclusive Communities Project, Inc., et al., deals with the idea of how to address [as if it were necessary] a "problem" called "disparate impact" about which the U.S.

Department of Housing and Urban Development recently issued an activist policy calling it, "Affirmatively Furthering Fair Housing."

In plain words, the government alleged, and the court agreed, by a single vote, that it has the authority to socially re-engineer every American community by forcibly adjusting its ethnic composition, regardless of the fact that such "unequal" numerical distributions are:

> " not *designed, intended, or used* to discriminate because of race, color, religion, sex, or national origin." [see decision, dissent by Justice Thomas, p. 34]

If you think this might be a 21st century resurrection of the 1970s and 80s incredibly divisive issue of forced school busing to achieve [and utterly fail] at implementing an ephemeral policy establishing "racial neutrality" you would be correct. If not actively challenged, as was the busing scheme, the "Texas Department of Housing and Community Affairs" case will allow the federal government to essentially mandate where one might live and who one's neighbors might be - pity the communities in which the Fed deems in effect there aren't enough violent drug dealers or Islamic fanatics.

This decision allows the HUD/EEOC/FHA etc. to specifically target predominantly white suburban communities which naturally formed outside of the confines and as a response against high-crime violent inner cities inhabited primarily by people of color.

As Justice Alito stated in his dissent, especially regarding the statutory language of the Fair Housing Act:

> "The FHA is not ambiguous. The FHA prohibits only disparate treatment, not disparate impact. It is a bedrock rule that an agency can never 'rewrite clear statutory terms to suit its own sense of how the statute should operate.' This rule makes even more sense where the agency's view

would open up a deeply disruptive avenue of liability that Congress never contemplated. Not only does disparate-impact liability run headlong into the text of the FHA, it also is irreconcilable with our precedents." [see decision, dissent by Justice Alito, joined by the Chief Justice, Justice Scalia and Justice Thomas, p. 60-61

Additionally, Justice Thomas assailed what he views as an overbroad application of a previous case, Griggs v. Duke Power Co.:

"Griggs' disparate-impact doctrine defies not only the statutory text, but reality itself. In their quest to eradicate what they view as institutionalized discrimination, disparate-impact proponents doggedly assume that a given racial disparity at an institution is a product of that institution rather than a reflection of disparities that exist outside of it." [see dissent, Justice Thomas, p. 36]

Despite a total lack of evidence that there was any intent to discriminate against protected classes [because it didn't exist] the fact that it failed to align with the statistical bias in HUD's metric now makes it actionable. Shockingly, according to the ruling the plaintiff only has the responsibility of establishing a prima facie case of "disparate impact" upon which the defendant is then essentially found guilty unless it can be proven that some overriding, exculpatory mitigating purpose can be established.

The larger question contrasts equality of opportunity - one of the bed rock principals of the nation - against equality of outcome, which is only possible in a totalitarian system. This is true because people have a limit to how much of their property they will allow the central government to expropriate without rising in direct, possibly violent, opposition.

Using the government's fuzzy logic in other areas demonstrates the absurdity of the underlying principle in that if applied generally throughout the society - and there is no indication this is not the ultimate intent - then income must be evenly distributed across the United States, regardless of any extenuating factors. In which case the fact that ethnic minorities tend to make less than Caucasians and Asians is proof of a subliminal racism that the Feds will have the power to address.

The increasingly shrill denunciations by Marxists and their newest allies the Christo-socialists such as Pope Francis - along with the majority of the Catholic Church's clerical superstructure - against "income inequality" should serve as adequate warning to American traditionalists who believe [as did the Founders] that success is obtained by the sweat of one's brow, not on a dole from Big Brother underwritten by governmental larceny and class-warfare inspired greed and envy.

Also at center-stage in this battle between DC's bureaucracy and the American Golden Goose - capitalism - is the difficulty of the culture to defend itself against huge federal bureaucracies - comprised of unelected individuals [which according to the Civil Service Act, essentially have tenure for life regardless of their misdeeds] - which inexorably seek to expand their sphere of influence and control, thus having a steadily corrosive effect on liberty and freedom.

In drawing down, we present what might be called the "San Bernardino Effect" referring to horrific act of jihad perpetrated at a local government office building by Tashfeen Malik and Syed Rizwan Farook which resulted in the death of 14.

Such operations rarely go completely unnoticed by the locals.

Interviewed subsequently, neighbors reported odd things happening in and around the jihadist's residence. Numerous comings and goings at unusual hours, frenetic activity in the couple's garage, the type of suspicious activity which is often associated with criminal behavior.

Yet the warning signs were intentionally ignored, the observers, rightly thinking in the current environment [especially that of California, which is gleefully morphing into the equivalent of the last of the Soviet Socialist "Republics"] that calling it to the attention of law enforcement might subject them to charges of racism, bigotry and Islamophobia. As per the design of the Muslim Brotherhood and its coven of leftist supporters, once again the unholy alliance made the act of self-defense itself a very dicey proposition.

Societies which fail or refuse to defend themselves invariably perish.

CHAPTER ELEVEN - THERE WILL BE CONSEQUENCES

If you rise in opposition to what has and continues to take place you will - if nothing else - be labeled generically as a "hater," as risible that as that term is under these circumstances. It's a vituperative, all-encompassing phrase used to stigmatize those for whom the transformationalists haven't yet constructed a specific pejorative. The goal of these people is to criminalize dissent to what Robert Bork [who had a rather intimate understanding of the process of destroying people politically] called <u>Slouching Towards Gomorrah</u> and indicative of what Allan Bloom argued in, <u>The Closing of the American Mind</u>.

With the former counter culture - allied with its fellow radical Muslims - having so thoroughly infiltrated the governmental infrastructure, the entire weight of the state is already being used as a club against dissenters by way of a highly selective application of "justice." Once the targeting coordinates are selected, in short order huge legal fees accrue to those caught in the crosshairs. Arrayed against these "enemies of the state," could well be hundreds of salaried investigators, attorneys, prosecutors and the like.

If the defendant wins, the victory is hollow, as the cost of a successful defense can easily bankrupt [by design] even the largest enterprises. The counter strategy for the innocent then becomes to seek a plea bargain in order to avoid the worst of the draconian consequences. Often this is in the form of an enormous fine, a "settlement," "mitigation," or as it's called on the street, a shakedown for protection money.

This is the great evil - very much like an auto-immune disease - which now confronts the nations of the no-longer "Free World," which are quickly losing their vitality and cultural confidence. The process is unfolding in an atmosphere in which Western tradition is not only under continuous assault but has lost the will to defend itself for numerous reasons, one of which sadly, is because a significant plurality have been convinced that the "system," our very way of life, isn't worth fighting for.

Another aspect of this are the real world examples of how people's lives are ruined by standing for tradition against the culture warriors incessant full-court press.

The disintegration of societal cohesion is quickened as older generations are naturally replaced by those coming up through the ranks, those who don't see America through their elders' eye. More fully explained, whereas generational change is inevitable, as the gray beards drift into obscurity they also take with them the traditions upon which the republic has relied for so long; but the environment has changed so quickly and radically that as the fresh upstarts work their way through the educational system they become acclimated to a mythical country which bears little resemblance to a certifiable reality. These students are intentionally being deprived of their history, which through countless examples testifies as to the basic goodness of Western Civilization and its efforts to self-correct the types of injustices which all human societies have. Instead - under the influence for example of ahistorical "history" texts written by leftist, bomb-throwing zealots such as Howard Zinn - they're taught the opposite, that the West is based upon a voracious imperialistic capitalism which has stolen the riches of the world for itself.

Because this type of pedagogy is designed more with indoctrination in mind rather than education, many of the millennials lack the most basic of critical thinking skills. What is there to think about anyway, since the truth is written on the left's equivalent of the Ten Commandments?

This is a decoupling process that destroys any sense of continuity, of being part of a larger, more grand and exceptional experience which in itself has merit. Engaging in the defense of traditional America under such constraints comes at great cost. The result, as we witness every day, is tragic. In academic environments the leftist cant is so rigidly enforced that even students who disagree with the radicalism of their often demonstrably half-witted professors, toe the party line because they know that dissent within the classroom is uniformly punished with a heavy thumb on the grading scale.

In a more concrete sense, the attack on Western culture takes place in a world which - through a seasoned set of eyes - is oft times not recognizable, where, as noted in the last chapter, self-defense itself has become illegal. If one dare [rightly] conclude in some public manner that terrorism and Islam are inextricably linked and one escapes with only an abject and scowling denial - the default and frankly moronic response will always be, "well every group has its bad players, we can't judge them all by the actions of one" - a very different mentality than the World War I battle cry which was even on the lips of school children, 'I will not be a slacker; I will kill the Huns.'

In the current environment there can never be reasonable justification for law enforcement to "profile" the usual suspects at airports [as do the Israelis quite successfully] or surveil mosques preaching violence-tainted, subversive hatred, which any sane society should do.

Thus the frightening prospect emerges; even thinking in these terms is rapidly approaching the Orwellian status of "thoughtcrime."

Irrespective of the societal and political push and shove, these and related issues will ultimately be adjudicated in a setting which has undergone these same profound changes as has the rest of the culture. When a single jurist on the U.S. Supreme Court can, unalterably, change the country overnight, something is terribly wrong.

Israel's imperious high court has taken this type of behavior to such extraordinary extremes that it has in large part usurped the legislative as well as the executive power and though the United States isn't quite there yet... it's racing to catch up.

In failing to challenge ascendant, confident and highly aggressive ideologies we allow mortal enemies to convince us to put the gun to our own collective head and pull the trigger. A vital constituency within what is left of the "old order" as well as the brash young upstarts have been intentionally deceived into believing that the culture is cancerous. That this critique is leveled from the lap of the most decent, affluent and generous society history has yet produced only adds to the irony.

Even strong, resilient societies will not long thrive if they allow themselves to be destroyed through the abuse of the very freedoms which define them in the first place, thus, "sabotaging its miserable house by their own hand."

When nations lose their souls, their days are numbered.

What complicates the battle to preserve the West is that so few really have any grasp of the dimensions or the stakes involved in the conflict. This isn't about seeking marginal political advantage, nor is it about dissident groups out to secure a greater voice within society.

Islamism and Cultural Marxism aren't partisan entities and share no part of the classical liberal tradition.

What they represent are sacralized, religiously framed ideologies held by individuals who are in the truest sense of the word, fanatics, whose entire existence is built around their core beliefs. These are people with whom no accommodation is possible; they are immune to traditional Western methods of peaceful conflict resolution. They want no part of the negotiating table and aren't in the least interested in incrementalism except as a waypoint on the road to total victory - Mohammed's *hudna* or calculated, tactical ceasefire.

There is nothing "soft" about the tyranny that they are quickly erecting around us. What is envisioned for the Western democracies are full-blown totalitarian police states indistinguishable from those of Nazi Germany, the Soviet Union or Mao's Red China.

Yes, perhaps the trains will run on time and the ultimate social justice ideal of equality of outcome might be generally enforced through a forced sharing of universal misery. But there will be consequences, dissidents to the new social order will ride those same rail cars to the inevitable factories of death as did Jewish Germans, mid-20th century, or in the best case, brutal "reeducation" camps.

Once set along this path there is no other destination possible.

Yet, there are those who maintain the fire of freedom and liberty against the onset of the maelstrom, even in Europe which is preceding us in the race towards the abyss.

A few years ago Swiss MP Oskar Freysinger made a speech in Berlin, touching upon some of the issues dealt with in the book which the reader now holds in his hands.

Though hopeful, it seems that it is with a wistful sense of resignation that Mr. Freysinger approaches the only question that matters any longer. Please keep in mind that though he is specifically dealing with Islamism, in a very real sense he is speaking metaphorically about the allied forces which are hastening our demise:

"Europe is an idea, a cultural landscape, an intellectual space shaped by history. Europe is the cradle of the modern constitutional democracy, the treasure house of human rights, of freedom of opinion and expression. Or at least it used to be that...until recently. It has increasingly been put into danger as our political elite bend their necks before a certain religious dogma which is completely alien to our intellectual history, our values and rule of law.

This dogma is gnawing away at the pillars of our system of laws, wherever it is granted the space to do so. This dogma demands total obedience of its followers. They should never integrate into our system of values. That would be "treason" to them and is punishable by death. They are supposed to conquer and subdue our Western world, not with tanks, rockets or riflemen, something they could never accomplish anyway. Not through brutal revolt. No, Islam is in no hurry it has an eternity, a long process of demoralization and slow motion occupation of our weakened child-poor society is foreseen.

The Islamic doctrine is intended to creep into our everyday life bit by bit and make Fortress Europe crumble from within. Just think of how the Serbs lost Kosovo. Through demographic development and the help of NATO which aided the founding of the first Islamic state of European soil...And what are we doing? We are allowing this violent doctrine in to subvert our rule of law, wholly unhindered in our cultural ghettos. Have we gone mad?

We just shrug our shoulders when girls are forced into marriage and integrated Muslims are pressured and threatened. And we look the other way as the women are beaten and whole city districts taken over. We think we can soften the power-lusting "holy warriors" with social benefits. We think we can buy our way to peace of mind.

What lunacy.

The prophet's beard is not for fondling. Fanatics cannot be bought. Germany should know this, more so than any other country in the world. My dear friends in the audience we are not fighting against people, we are fighting for people. We are fighting against a dogma that despises all humanity and wants to push us back into barbarity.

We will not easily give up the freedom for which we have fought so hard over the centuries.

Dear Berliners, here I stand, because no one in Europe will stand up even for the very pillar of our civilization, our rule of law, our humanity. The transcendental, unconditional, "Love thy neighbor," that is the pillar." [source, Excerpt of 2011 Speech in Berlin delivered by Swiss MP Oskar Freysinger]

But will the pillar prevail against the looming storm clouds?

Can something be done?

Pardon our skepticism, but it's rather late in the day to halt the process, let alone gear up into reactionary/counter-revolutionary mode, the only philosophy which has any possibility of wresting the culture back from those who are in the process of destroying it.

The longer this continues the greater will be the violence necessary to reverse it.

Don't delude yourself...this isn't 1776 by any means, the enemy isn't 3,000 miles away across an angry ocean, nor is he wearing a red coat and marching in a straight line. Those dozens of weapons secured in your safe, your generator, emergency food supply, cache of bullion and the rest, though good, proper and moral, pale against the threat.

The culture is wired and interdependent to a degree that Madison, Jefferson, Washington and Lincoln could never have imagined. Communication is instantaneous, surveillance is approaching total and those controlling the process aren't squeamish about invoking the horrific if that's what it takes.

This is the face of a genuine and ascendant existential threat. The nascent masters have but one demand: unconditional, abject surrender and they are ultimately prepared to make ISIS look like a girl scout picnic in order to secure it.

By all measures the crises of the West has moved beyond the entreaties of simple traditional conservatism. Actually for all intents and purposes conservatism as most envision it might as well receive an honorable burial because it is most certainly dead. How can a society stand strong and firm in the face of endless - albeit microscopic - surrenders, of an endless pattern of concessions hoping to find some sort of common ground with which to buy off the leftist/Islamist coalition, whose lexicon does not contain the word compromise.

In this sense conservatism has failed, not just because it's the wrong prescription for our level of decay - an inherent defect in the theory, but also because its self-styled handmaidens have proven themselves cowards looking out only for their short-term interests, oblivious to the fact that they are just pushing an ever more malignant threat down the road a piece.

Believe it, the Founders were much more than what the sterile term conservatism implies; having a clear and deep understanding of their heritage [which we of course, by extension, share with them] going back to the Greek philosophers, in the end they had the insight, wisdom, pragmatic judgment and strength of purpose to fight for it.

Recalling the first verse of Yeats' dystopian post World War I era poem, "The Second Coming."

> "Turning and turning in the widening gyre
> The falcon cannot hear the falconer;
> Things fall apart; the centre cannot hold;
> Mere anarchy is loosed upon the world,
> The blood-dimmed tide is loosed, and everywhere
> The ceremony of innocence is drowned;
> The best lack all conviction, while the worst
> Are full of passionate intensity."

Morally, Western men and women have no choice; they can do nothing less than resist evil, it being the prime imperative of any time and place - whether it will do any good rests in the hands of the Almighty, if He has not already forsaken us.

CODA: SUBURBAN RHYTHM NODE

The SundayChron...once miraculous...now light bouncing off the surrounding lottery minefield.

The quartz Pyramid planted on Giannini's sarcophagus, fingering Allah, five-fifty-five California, Bernake's preserve...minting greenbacks already fading in fog-lit-sunlight.

The paper rolls in, stinking, smiling in its own filth...Gramsci's dictum...march soldiers, march...through institutions beyond shriveled comprehension, hands now agrip the wheel.

Did you see my Garmin?

Yet that rag remains both a joyous vision and a keyholed stepladder to the lowest depths of Hell. It entertains, deforms, hard news on wry, bracketed between the keepers of the faith.

Opera square dystopia. Penguins with sequined vapid fleshtoys, appendages easily disposed of, then reacquired as needed...self-regenerating starfish.

The crime report feloniously masking minority perps. They differ, they bicker, they kick you in the balls, yet you buy...a four-bit a day habit, lovely inky trackmarks coursing up the thigh.

Awards drift by, the CNPA...assclowns, sometimes getting it right, but always inadvertently. They aggregate, congregate, parasitically liplocked to the Times, the WashPost all in mysterious editorial goosestep.

I love Her. There...I said it and did not self combust. Like falling for a whore, its appeal, animal. Ignore that ice cold tingle of impending, endless darkness...you are drawn in, you must enter.

Raised by the printed word which rode upon the pen of Caen, Delaplane, Hoppe and the town's Irish drunk, McCabe. It must have slowly metastasized into my DNA, a cradle addict. The town's bars and diners were tightly bound around some in this bunch.

Mighty Caen travelled gratis.

Blight on you mister restaurateur...barkeep...city hall hack on some other guy's take. Broken winged social butterfly, do not incur his wrath...public flaying is sharp and nasty.

A daily injection of prose, telepathically orchestrating the rhythm and flow of the city. With anticipation you awaited that muffled black morning thud in the suburban driveway, next to the white Malibu wagon, three in the tree, manual steering and drum brakes of questionable performance.

Natty bowler-hatted Charles McCabe, a culture writer streaming his fancies, irks, despairs. Don't rile him early son...alky-head throbbing notions set in lead.

Though his death cert did not proclaim it, he was on the frontier, felled by the first wave of Nazi synaptic controllers. Who could realize it, pilings slowly eaten away...and by what?

Grubs, insects assembled by pasty-faced wired codesmiths, crushed and emptied cans of Red Bull littered about.

A different flavored smugness then. No more the perfume of Hams brewery, its glaring clarion toppled and forgotten, cardboard broken, edges frayed. Gone the coffee roasters, Yuban, that hefty cup that woke the city.

A 60s visit to the Hams brewery aside my father...before OSHA's cord was severed, before the iron grasp of the feudal lords and ladies.

You had to have your wits about you at Hams - riding from one level of the plant to the next clinging to an endlessly revolving bronc of a vertical levitator. Step, quickly, step off boy. The hose patrol down there will wash away the inattentive from the cold tiles below...galvanized buckets in hand.

Hard men, vets of countless wars cracking a few on the job, who could blame them? I was special that day, in a chalice they offered me to drink...blue green fluorescence gently swirling. But The Man interceded, not wasting a drop of the precious bubbly, downing it with practiced hand...a satisfying gurgle like sound.

Disheveled and grimy, a charming door to Midwestern belching industrial might, it didn't repel, it put you at ease, it was organic, alive like garden tilth or sometimes like that dog shit you scrape off your soles while softly cursing.

They bled in, earnest love children dragging the steely edge of drug music culture behind them.

A chasm, opened, old America...new Amerika.

One hand nurtures, its twin...destroyer of worlds.

Could we have read the signposts, sniffed the air...known what was coming? Or were we frozen in the beautiful Beat Poet days, Ginsberg, Ferlinghetti, Orolovsky, all fey...and City Lights Bookstore...musty aroma and cheap incense.

Howl, Sunflower Sutra, A Way Above a Harborful, Death to Van Gogh's Ear, Dharma Bums on the lam, cheap Mexican weed, Mescaline, Lysergic Acid and...later, Thompson's hideous Igobaine, extracted from the still warm pineals of babes. All this, flooding up from the undertow...imbuing...the wordplay a windowpane refraction.

Of no concern to the many, who were after all, perhaps right.

No Grecian oracle could have birthed a Twitter, a Facebook or...the Googleplex, itself...immovable, unknowable, all controlling...Sphinxlike.

Don't Be Evil..how tragic...

Nothing of import happens within the expanding tentacular universe of the mediakultur, a mass orgy of mindless, un-erotic Zuckerbergian masturbation.

Harvard's crafty revenge.

Google saintly Mark...and behold the uni, WillieBrown divined it from inside a fortune cookie...Kiton or Loro Piana blazer, jeans tailored so as not to be tailored, hand built Stefamo Bemer lace-ups.

With pride they waste these calloused artisans' love objects...the wooden lasts, the aroma of leather, animal glue and machine oil.

Italian, without the grace. Hateful one-percenters feeding on each other, occupying the occupiers, fanning the fires of their own penitential self-immolation.

They rise, plastic Christs on Easter morn ascending Mount Tam as California implodes, bestride the overseer...Savior, Leveler, ant-farm Balkanizer.

Surfing on the backs of those whom they despise...but depend on. Early morning mowing sounds, mad leaf blowers...turbines spinning impossibly fast, squeegees streaking across bulletproof glass 30 lifetimes high...they sleep on, plotting even in their dreams.

Can the princely few survive without their retinue? Deprived of their Mestizos, angry Caucasians, theses in hand, spitting in their patron's Glenlivets

Will this island of one channel brilliance be of sufficient mass to forge a pathway clear?

White ghetto housing...cubicle dwellers. the island divided, vivisectioned and dotted with tiny outposts of black hole import, all is breathed in. The Indians are coming, the barricades thin, powder dry, they gambol on - the gilted few.

The big armed lads have slipped away, their engine drone strangled. With them the upwards steppingstone too.

New and clammy fingers whirring, leaking strange brewed symbols.

Malware now, not smoking risered majesty.

Where the fuck is Rosie? Did she set her rivets free or did they mutiny?

Pierced tongue babes. spreadlegged by night. So wan, tangled spirits peering through bony hips..that pink maw, gaping.

Toothy smiles, too perfect.

Greedheads gazing through mirrored eyes, they are the ones they wanted. Why are they screaming not enough...not nearly enough? Slouching in scabrous towns of ripstop nylon, streets palleted against the ooze...muck squeezing up, some earthen urban waffle...libidinous squishy sounds.

Free Mumia, yes, free him now...free them all.

Jail the jailers, the animals grow restless.

What would H Rap do?

Drill cops through the spine?

Hit the street motherfucker, you're going down hard
...deadweight falling...

The thinblueones, lips pursed, such pretty mouths, entwined in the web too. On ghost watch - do not engage, that is an order. A thousand lies stare back.

Prelude or delicate gavotte? Curtsey as you quickly pass, glassy peanut brittle crunching under Doc Martens.

Don't rile the natives, turn the other cheek - that one's bleeding, sutured...why not own a pair?

Medic...morphine...

Run.

Run, mount the silvertrain to the East. HAL on the tinny speakerbox, next stop-Fruitvale Ave.

Eject, eject.

Sanctuary in one hundred blocks of Oaktown. This jungle, its rules, no quarter.

Push this one, it shoves back.

The chunky sound of a Glock going into battery...toetag in deep freeze at Highland...but dontchuknow its doors are chained?

But...that's the beauty isn't it?

Asian mayors make the most ironic fools, don't you think?

Clarabelle with huge red shoes behind a dim-sum cart off Broadway, no, duckfoot, not for whiteman. She cackles, like chicken. Rubber nose between your asscheeks...stay out of my cheerios. Hey the Doc's cobrasnakething steth needs counsel too, whisper to him...it will be fine, not broken at all.

Listen, the diaphragm instructs wisely.

Take two hours and call the aspirin in the morning.

Dammit, that makes the most sense. 60 milligrams b.i.d., always constant ever steady..cool off, it's just going 'round.

Gentle Blue Light herb cafe smashed by the Feds, breaching rounds in a Remington 870..rack that baby and you will silence the baddest of asses. On, on to Oaksterdam now, give my regards to Broadway.

The hard hand to come...this is your final warning.

Listenup people, of course its legal...bought your card...but someone needs a lesson.

You're an egg...DC needs omelets.

No, no, no...over there. That's him, natty doo-raged Holder, stiffest blackman in town, skipping the scene behind the wheel of a '65 Riviera. Don't be silly, sure he's the rubber-gloved triggerman. Check out the crease in his pants.

Man in Plaid gone rough...cat tongue rasping bone.

Run a make...carbon footprints match, case dismissed, let's play hoops.

Throw an elbow for the Gipper, chuck the Queen a Churchill bronze...too heavy for this bunch...leaking through the hallways late at night, taunting...a constant reminder.

Are those tears? Big dead bronzes don't cry...

The living deadboys dozing at the Ciscoswitches, dreaming a valley immaculately conceived in some siliconed womb beyond the reach of Packard or Hewlett's majic dick. It now commands its own patent office. Convenient logic...perfect.

Why not?

Retrain everyone, bind them to plastic chairs with grayducttape...array them with Teutonic precision. Is there any doubt that assembly line labor can engineer tomorrow with a keyboard?

Hurry, the bandwagon is rolling, there's always room for one more...for you. Look to the past, field workers make excellent physicians...make thatched roof house call in monsoon.

Uncle Mao did it.

Castro does it...though now locked in cancer's deadly embrace, along with Hugo, oddly the peasant healers have not been consulted for a second opinion, their time must be too valuable.

How else to explain? Such self sacrifice will not go unrewarded, even in this world turned inside out.

It's knocking now...look, Clarabelle at a presser today, LaHood and Brown at her side, but not too close, no, bad form...what if this beast crashes before they leave the stage?

Emptymouthed grants Oaktown's jigsawed container port will never see.

ChiCom nukes sifting in.

Look for the union label, now that would be real progress...that banker's call, stiff armed for months...the rust encrusted infrastructure is sold off for scrap, not likely to return, except maybe recycled into sewer grates.

Hey you, don't dump that here, can't you read? The sintered placard murmuring...I drain to the Bay...take your corrupted Pennzoil elsewhere...the county feeds on toxic waste, only blood must flow to the sea, keep it organic stupid.

Simple street smarts...taste and see...betcha can't just eat one...

Thou shalt kill, rape, burn, maim, destroy, it is so written...free yourselves from the colonial oppressors...brothers and sisters, embrace your inner Oscar Grant, ink him on CDX.

Crucify him on 7th & Madison, next to Chinese deadduck on hook.

Oh...come let us adore him...on every shattered downtown window.

Thy faith hath saved ye...Oscar arise.

Belief...this is the fire next time. Now doctor, tell me, is that habit forming?

High on psycho violence, razor wire not seen since jarheads meatground their way through Fallujah...those dead don't clean up so pretty now do they? And what of the ashen tatters jetted off to Ramstein? IV tubing, paper tape, reddening Kerlix sponges ...Steri Drapes...stainless trays...bonesaw slaughterhouse implements.

What of them? Heroes so precious we hide them inside a box at which we throw bags of last year's underwear.

Hey Oaktown...dogcollared cops...down boy that's none of your concern...here go reason with the ripstop tentpeople, let them know you too are allies, down with the man, we are the man...down with us then...what's a little more self hate...they aspire to it...bankers hours and hollow pensions.

But observe...their ranks are tightly packed though canned and sardined, always at the ready for the dispatch that will never come.

That fuse will blow.

You sense the vacant gambit. Indemnification...easily purchased.

Confessor...my indulgence? So what truster? Milk the tit of daddy's belief...better that way, you sure as hell can't stack the Legos...but you learn...yes access that third eye...those who do not can't comprehend the guide wires...

What joy.

Is it the secret handshake? Maybe they just covet your red Porsche. Smugness, now virtuous...speak truth to the empiric enemy...till the fields of noble intent...earnest-pride softens the fall, means and deadends.

This, from which omniscience flows...art-history greasing combine bearings...and the happy clones, Netgearheads aren't of this world...they cohabit with others, clawing out of the thin parchment cells in the same hive, wings drying,...pumping...one of many stacked worlds of alternate realities which intersect at the nodes where the cash changes hands.

Infused now they soar...chainsaw sound...always grinding, wearing away the paledead prehistory.

Strata by strata, metamorphic atop igneous...magma thickly flowing, syrup like below. Fissures and fault lines

With subductive certainty we are undone.

But are we?

Is this rebirth or is this the really the end?

My God man how can it end now, that's just not cricket I say, no not at all...mad dogs, Englishmen and all that topped by a pint of warm Guinness.

Now that is a travesty of the first order.

Are we being newly minted, molded from some plasticene jello like substance, ever malleable...one size fits all?

The standardized man, some assembly required. The manufacturer will not assume responsibility for misuse of the product. No warranty expressed or implied.

You are on your own brother, how does that feel? An errant breeze at your back, the late Summer sun setting over Grizzly Peak, fog rolling in, a masterpiece. Do not corral it, break it of its spirit.

It's more than form, more than substance more than it appears, but maybe less than is required, who knows what is needed?

If that were the case then Hostess could fashion it out of honey colored spongebread filled with foamy white stuff resembling cream, but with a shelf life measured in eons...

INDEX

Adams, John Quincy, a Founding Father's critique of Islam, especially its non spiritual nature, 46-47

Adams, Samuel, requirements to retain liberty, 6

Akram, Mohammed, author, *The General Strategic Plan for the Group in North America*, 35

Al-Bana, Hasan, founder, Egyptian Muslim Brotherhood, 37

Al-Shabaab, atrocities, 72

Ali, Ayan Hirsi, script consultant, van Gogh film, *Submission*, 16

American Civil Liberties Union [ACLU]:
and lawfare, 104
partnering with Islamists, 118

Arafat, Yasser, "Palestine" created to support Islamic expansionism and destruction of Israel, 122

Arendt, Hannah, *Hannah Arendt: Critical Essays*, Edited by Lewis P. Hinchman and Sarah K. Hinchman, p. 217,
suppression of individuality in service of creating a "group" identity, thus making all complicit in the crimes of the state, 130

Arjomand, Said Amir, *Revolution, Critical Concepts in Political Science*, 63

Assad, Hafez al-Assad, "Palestine," an entirely political construction, 122

Babbit, Irving, spiritual strength of closely held ideologies, 42,

Detroit, city of, 28

Dewey, John, PhD, among the first of the progressive intellectuals, 151

Dostoevsky, Fyodor, *The Brothers Karamazov*, p 71

Elashi, Ghassan, CAIR Texas kingpin, convicted in U.S. v. Holy Land Foundation, 33

Ellery, William, 3

Ellison, Keith [D-MN], 166-167

Elliott, Jonathan, *Journal and Debates, a History of the Federal Constitution*, 8

Emanuel, Rahm, former Obama Chief of Staff, exploitation of crises, 105

Engels, Friedrich, *Das Kapital*, 48

Emerson, Steven, Investigative Project on Terrorism:
Muslim Brotherhood influence peddling in the White House, 34
on CAIR claim conflation "War on Terror" with "War on Islam," 107

Farook, Syed Rizwan, and San Bernardino jihad, 175

Fodor, Jerry A., Phd, *The Language of Thoughts Revisited*, 100

Fortuyn, Pym, 13-16

Franklin, Benjamin, 3, 6

Freud, Sigmund, *Civilization and its Discontents*, 58

Freysinger, Oskar, MP Switzerland, 181-183

Google:
McLuhan's theories writ large, information filtering, 134
gatekeeper effect, 142

Gramsci, Antonio:
general introduction, Marxist cultural modeling, identification
with Lenin's dual power concept, *Prison Notes*, and Yuri
Bezmenov, and multiculturalism, theories in practice, 71-79
as represented in actions of Trevor Phillips, 85
and lexicon, 100, 102
and Lenin, 126
pertaining to McLuhan, 142
regarding cultural defense, 169

Grenville, George, British Prime Minister, 41

Gutenberg, Johannes, originator of movable type printing,
historic impact regarding glyphic communication, the ancient
oral tradition, democratization of knowledge, 156-137

Haidt, Jonathan, PhD, *The Righteous Mind*, social psychologist,
the structure of political beliefs, 29

HAMAS, 33, 34, 70, 106, 120, 156

Hegel, Georg Wilhelm Friedrich, historicism as an influence on
Marx, 67-68,
and Progressives, 151

Heller, Peter:
false claims regarding wolf population in Yellowstone Park, 111
revealed as enviro-activist, 112

Hitler, Adolph, 25, 158

Holy Land Foundation prosecution, 33-24
Aand CAIR, 105

Hofstadgroep, 16

Hoover, J. Edgar, former Director of the FBI, and Martin Luther King, 92

Hume, David, *Treatise on Being*, 30

Industrial Revolution, 49

Islamic Circle of North America [ICNA], ally of Muslim Brotherhood, 36

Islamic Society of North America [ISNA], HAMAS associated Muslim Brotherhood front group, unindicted co-conspirator/joint venturer in U.S. v. Holy Land Foundation, 33-34

ISIS, 33, 35, 72, 183

Jade Helm 15, U.S. Federal government, specifically SOCOM community trains in anticipation of domestic civil unrest, 127

Jefferson, President Thomas, Founding Father:
as author of the Declaration of Independence, 5
referencing "nature's God", 72
assailed by Woodrow Wilson, 151
Founding Father, author of *The Declaration of Independence*, 6

Johns Hopkins University, importing the German, leftist pedagogic model, 150-151

Kerry, John, Financial Times 2004 presidential race, 20

King, Martin Luther:
journey from Christian pacifism to support for "wars of liberation, 91
and Communist Stanley Levison, 93-94

Kirk, Russell:
as popularize of 20th century conservatism, 39

anti-Semitism, ref., *The Geography of Hope, Exile, the Enlightenment, Disassimilation*, 67-68

Mawdudi, Abul, A'la, Pakistani revolutionary Islam, theory of jihad, duality of Islam, 62-63
Towards Understanding Islam, 65

Mayer, William:
Bitter Harvest: How "Progressives" Have Infiltrated the Catholic Church, 49
Occupy Wall Street Oakland, Taste the Madness, 156

McLuhan, Marshall, PhD, *The Gutenberg Galaxy*, effect of media in creating an enveloping corrosive global culture, the revolutionary nature of modern electronic communications and the Internet, the standardized man, 132-149

Menchu, Rigoberta:
I Rigoberta Menchu, 95
and false, but powerful cultural narratives, 96-99
further commentary on transformational parables, 115, 123
relevance to the vibrancy of admittedly false notions presented as certifiable truth, 160

Milgram, John, PhD, ground-breaking research regarding power relationships and authority figures, 54-55

Mohammed, as the "final" prophet, 44

Mohsen, Zuheir, "we are all part of one people, the Arab nation," 123

Morris, Robert, 4

Muslim Brotherhood, the:
and jihadist theory of Mohammed Bouyeri, 16
linkage to HAMAS, 34
and Mohammed Akram, 35
blueprint for "civilization jihad, 35-36

Parker, Captain John, Lexington Green, 10

PipeLineNews.org:
Holy Land Foundation prosecution, 34
referencing jihadist depravity, 72
Islamic refusal to acculturate, 80
myth of Islamophobia, 85, 153
"Flying" imams, 166

Plato:
and Socrates 22-25
and the theory of "the good," 58

Popper, Karl, PhD, philosophy of science, refutation of theories
which by design cannot be proven false, 153

Pope Francis, and Christo-socialism, 175

Pope Leo XIII, *Rerum Novarum*, gravely defective, error-filled
critique of Marxism, 49

Phillips, Trevor:
as popularizer of term Islamophobia, use of NGOs to attain
wealth and fame, transcript, official inquiry, 85-87

Rand, Ayn, *Atlas Shrugged*, capitalism vs. altruism, 52

Rawls, John, PhD, *A Theory of Justice, Justice is Fairness*,
defense of redistributionism and multiculturalism, 1154-155

Rodney, Caesar, 2

Ryan, Monsignor John August, *Distributive Justice*, 50-51

Shari'a, Islamic law, sources of authority, general references
such as in "Shari'a compliance," 16, 45, 61, 62, 109, 115, 161-
164, 171

Shakespeare, William, *The Twelfth Night*, 2

Socrates, 22

Solis, Jorge, Federal District Judge, judicial decisions subsequent to and regarding *U.S. v. Holy Land Foundation*, 34

Solomon, Chaim, 4

Stockton, Richard, 3

Students for a Democratic Society [SDS], 84

The Universal Declaration of Human Rights, 15

Torcello, Lawrence, PhD., "global warming denial," as criminality, 115

Trotsky, Leon:
permanent revolution, 75-76
within the pantheon of Marxist theorists, 84

Tubman, Harriet:
iconic imaging/registration regarding U.S. currency, role in bloody John Brown rebellion, 90

Tytler, Alexander Fraser, *From Bondage to Spiritual Faith*, 8-9

U.S. Supreme Court, *U.S. EEOC v. Abercrombie & Fitch*, 169-171, *Texas Department of Housing and Community Affairs et al. v. Inclusive Communities Project, Inc., et al.*, 172, *Griggs v. Duke Power*, 174

Van Gogh, Theo, Dutch film maker, polemicist, cultural gadfly, 11-21

Van Gogh, Vincent, 11

Van Haren, Lena, grade school indoctrination into multiculturalism and forced equally of result, 130

Waller, John, *A Forgotten Plague: Making Sense of Dance Mania*, Lancet Magazine, 125

Washington, President General George, Founding Father, 3, 4, 5, 7, 183

Wilson, President Woodrow, PhD, educator, the "living" Constitution, 151

Yeats, W.B., *The Second Coming*, 184

Zinn, Howard, PhD, *A People's History of the United States*, 178

ABOUT THE AUTHOR

William Mayer has had the pleasure of serving as the CEO/Editor & Publisher of the online national security newsletter, PipeLineNews.org LLC for the last seventeen years. He and his wife reside in the San Francisco Bay Area.

ISBN-13: 978-0692771945 (PipeLineMedia)
ISBN-10: 0692771948

83396499R00119

Made in the USA
Middletown, DE
11 August 2018